VOLUME 6

DELUXE GUITAR PLAY-ALONG

AUDIO ACCESS INCLUDED

RED HOT CHILI PEPPERS

(Cover photo by Gabriel Olsen/Getty Images)

PLAYBACK+
Speed · Pitch · Balance · Loop

To access audio visit:
www.halleonard.com/mylibrary

Enter Code
7440-8915-4359-3264

ISBN: 978-1-5400-0373-7

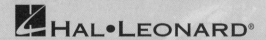

Visit Hal Leonard Online at
www.halleonard.com

Contact Us:
Hal Leonard
7777 West Bluemound Road
Milwaukee, WI 53213
Email: info@halleonard.com

In Europe contact:
Hal Leonard Europe Limited
Distribution Centre, Newmarket Road
Bury St Edmunds, Suffolk, IP33 3YB
Email: info@halleonardeurope.com

In Australia contact:
Hal Leonard Australia Pty. Ltd.
4 Lentara Court
Cheltenham, Victoria, 3192 Australia
Email: info@halleonard.com.au

GUITAR NOTATION LEGEND

THE MUSICAL STAFF shows pitches and rhythms and is divided by bar lines into measures. Pitches are named after the first seven letters of the alphabet.

TABLATURE graphically represents the guitar fingerboard. Each horizontal line represents a string, and each number represents a fret.

Notes:

Strings:
high E
B
G
D
A
low E

4th string, 2nd fret

1st & 2nd strings open, played together

open D chord

HALF-STEP BEND: Strike the note and bend up 1/2 step.

WHOLE-STEP BEND: Strike the note and bend up one step.

GRACE NOTE BEND: Strike the note and immediately bend up as indicated.

SLIGHT (MICROTONE) BEND: Strike the note and bend up 1/4 step.

BEND AND RELEASE: Strike the note and bend up as indicated, then release back to the original note. Only the first note is struck.

PRE-BEND: Bend the note as indicated, then strike it.

VIBRATO: The string is vibrated by rapidly bending and releasing the note with the fretting hand.

PALM MUTING: The note is partially muted by the pick hand lightly touching the string(s) just before the bridge.

HAMMER-ON: Strike the first (lower) note with one finger, then sound the higher note (on the same string) with another finger by fretting it without picking.

PULL-OFF: Place both fingers on the notes to be sounded. Strike the first note and without picking, pull the finger off to sound the second (lower) note.

LEGATO SLIDE: Strike the first note and then slide the same fret-hand finger up or down to the second note. The second note is not struck.

SHIFT SLIDE: Same as legato slide, except the second note is struck.

TRILL: Very rapidly alternate between the notes indicated by continuously hammering on and pulling off.

TAPPING: Hammer ("tap") the fret indicated with the pick-hand index or middle finger and pull off to the note fretted by the fret hand.

NATURAL HARMONIC: Strike the note while the fret-hand lightly touches the string directly over the fret indicated.

PINCH HARMONIC: The note is fretted normally and a harmonic is produced by adding the edge of the thumb or the tip of the index finger of the pick hand to the normal pick attack.

TREMOLO PICKING: The note is picked as rapidly and continuously as possible.

VIBRATO BAR DIVE AND RETURN: The pitch of the note or chord is dropped a specified number of steps (in rhythm), then returned to the original pitch.

VIBRATO BAR SCOOP: Depress the bar just before striking the note, then quickly release the bar.

VIBRATO BAR DIP: Strike the note and then immediately drop a specified number of steps, then release back to the original pitch.

Additional Musical Definitions

(accent) • Accentuate note (play it louder).

(staccato) • Play the note short.

D.S. al Coda • Go back to the sign (𝄋), then play until the measure marked "*To Coda*," then skip to the section labelled "**Coda**."

D.C. al Fine • Go back to the beginning of the song and play until the measure marked "*Fine*" (end).

Fill • Label used to identify a brief melodic figure which is to be inserted into the arrangement.

N.C. • Harmony is implied.

• Repeat measures between signs.

• When a repeated section has different endings, play the first ending only the first time and the second ending only the second time.

DELUXE GUITAR PLAY-ALONG

AUDIO ACCESS INCLUDED

RED HOT CHILI PEPPERS

The Adventures of Rain Dance Maggie

Words and Music by
Anthony Kiedis, Flea, Chad Smith and Josh Klinghoffer

Intro
Moderately ♩ = 106

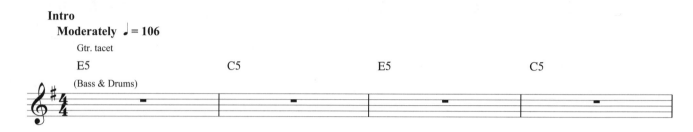

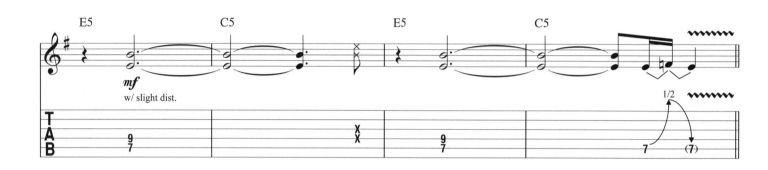

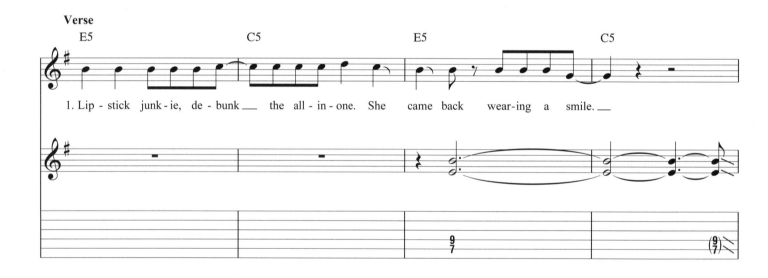

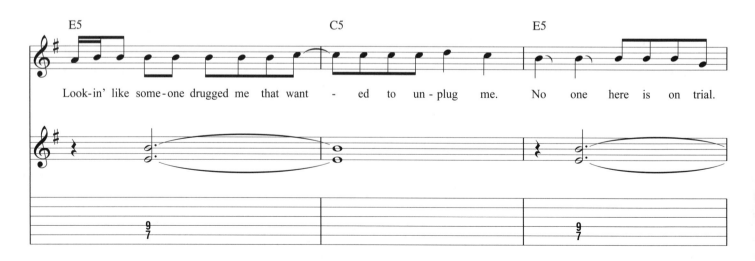

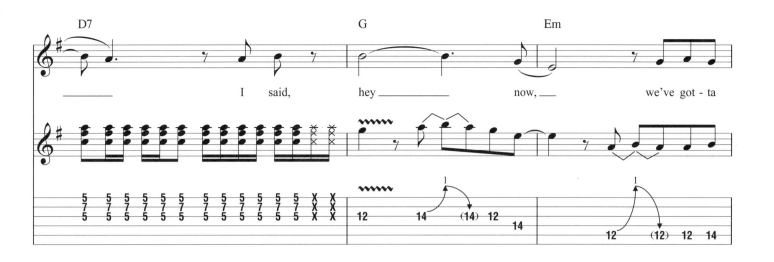

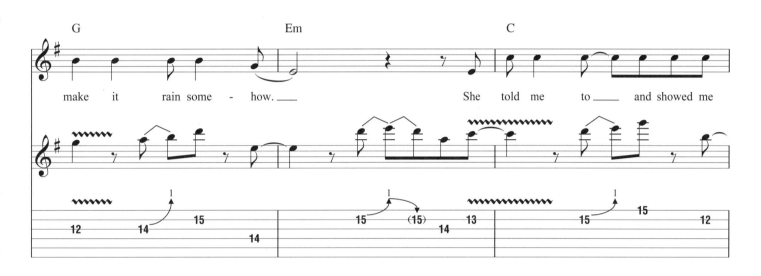

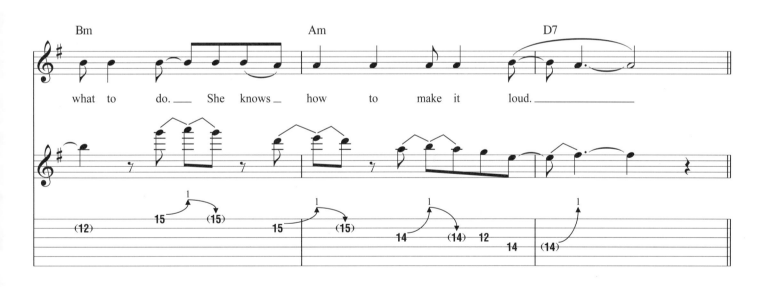

Interlude

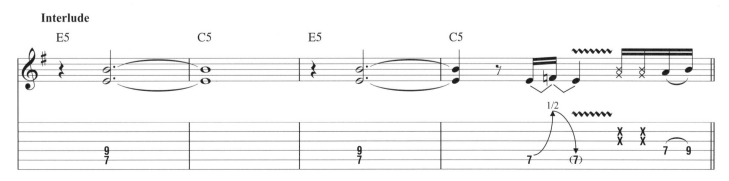

8

told me to _____ and showed me what to do. Our Mag - gie makes it in a cloud. ____

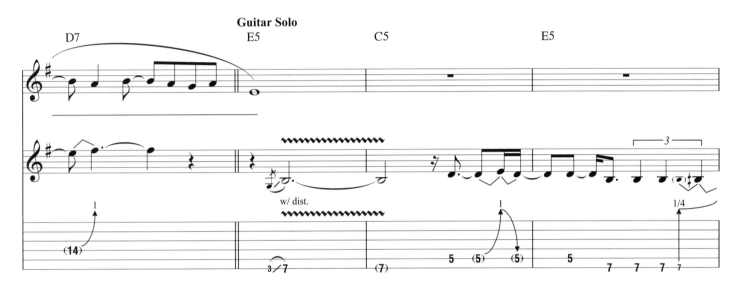

Guitar Solo

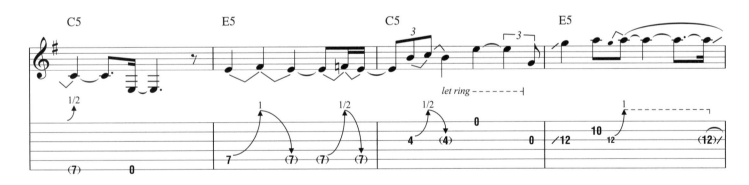

Bridge

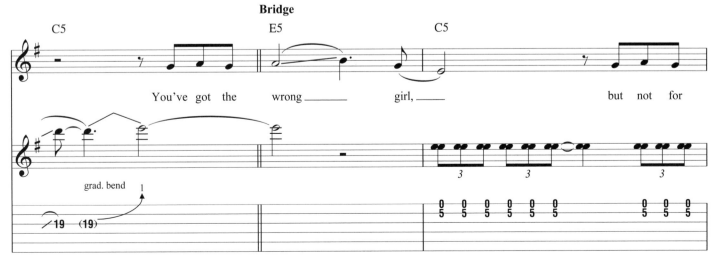

You've got the wrong _____ girl, _____ but not for

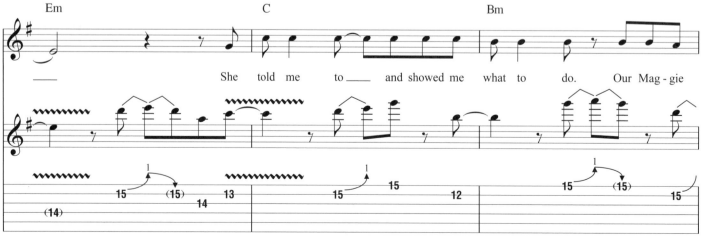

Breaking the Girl

Words and Music by Anthony Kiedis, Flea, John Frusciante and Chad Smith

Tune down 1/2 step:
(low to high) Eb-Ab-Db-Gb-Bb-Eb

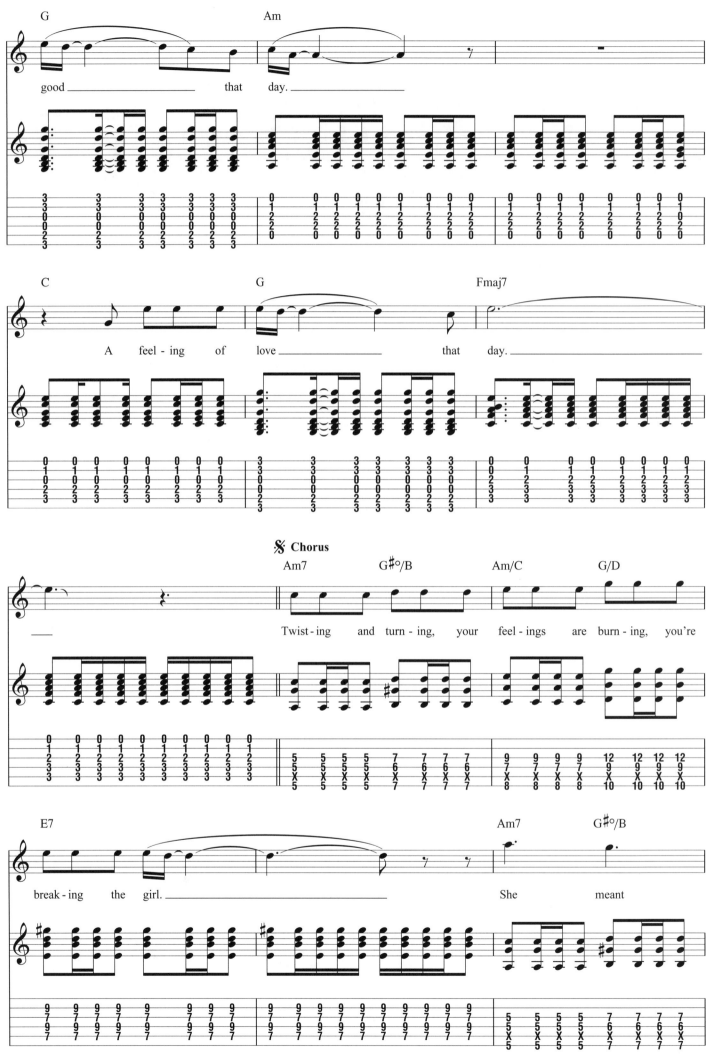

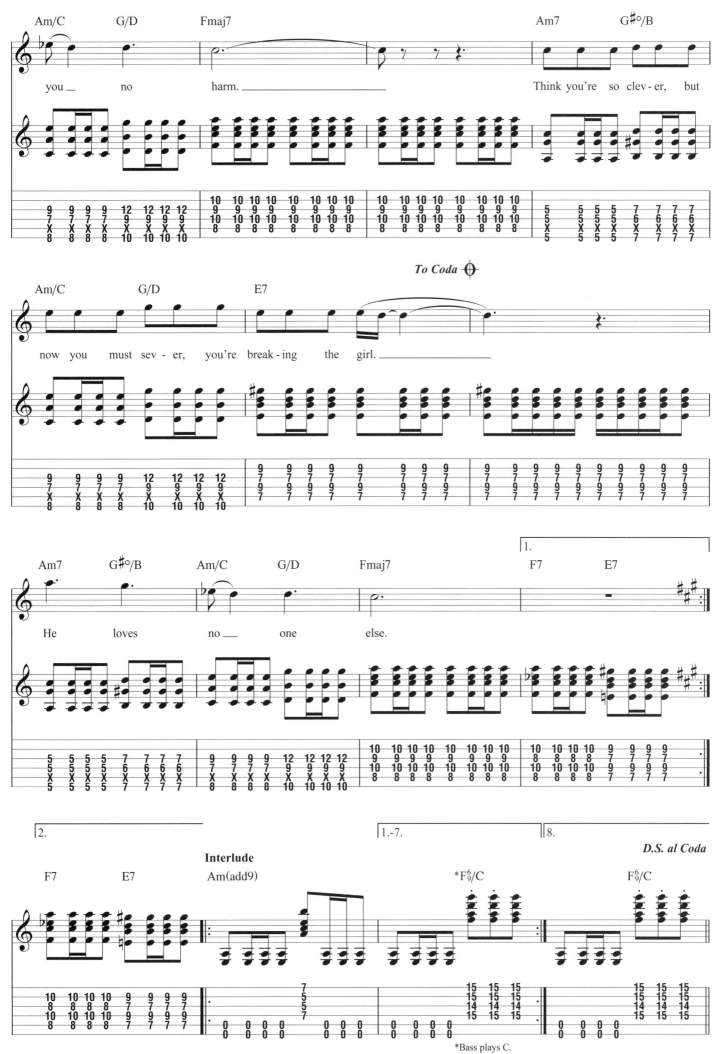

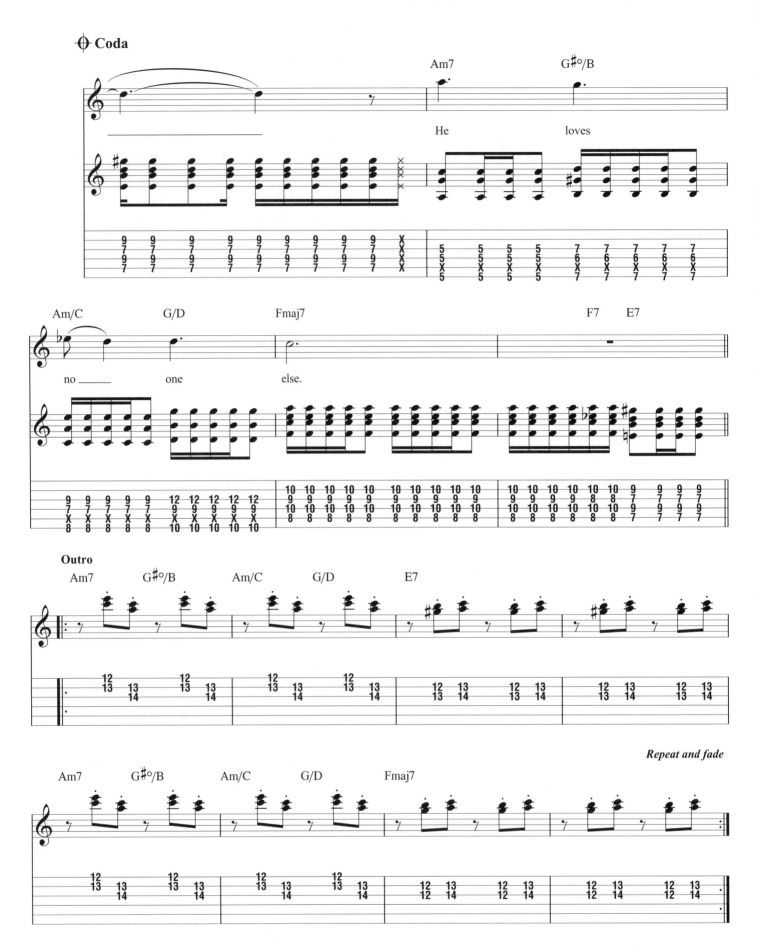

Additional Lyrics

2. Raised by my dad, girl of the day.
   He was my man, that was the way.
   She was the girl left alone.
   Feeling no need to make me her home.

Pre-Chorus I don't know what, when or why.
   The twilight of love had arrived.

Can't Stop

Words and Music by
Anthony Kiedis, Flea, John Frusciante and Chad Smith

Intro
Slow Funk-Rock ♩ = 88

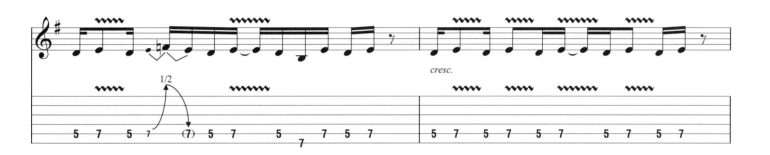

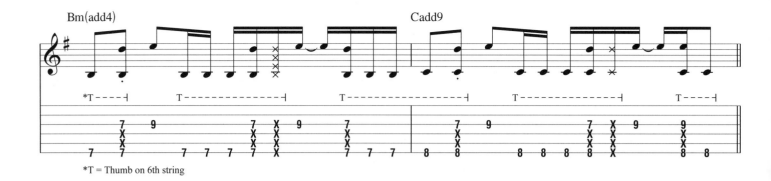

*T = Thumb on 6th string

Verse

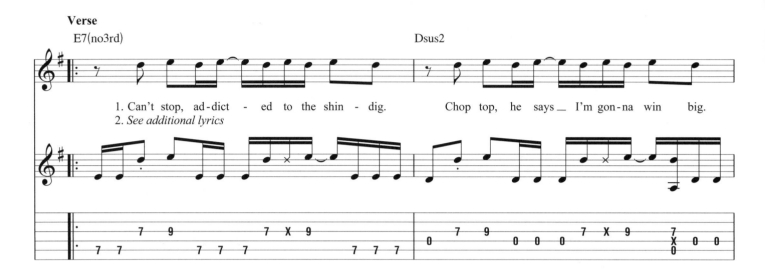

1. Can't stop, ad-dict - ed to the shin - dig. Chop top, he says __ I'm gon-na win big.
2. *See additional lyrics*

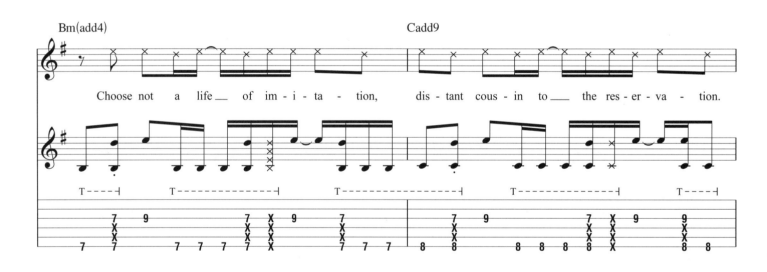

Choose not a life __ of im - i - ta - tion, dis - tant cous - in to __ the res - er - va - tion.

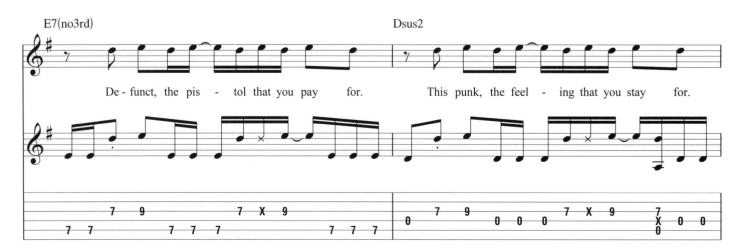

De - funct, the pis - tol that you pay for. This punk, the feel - ing that you stay for.

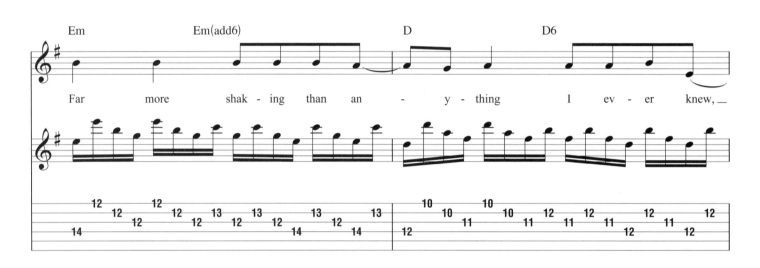

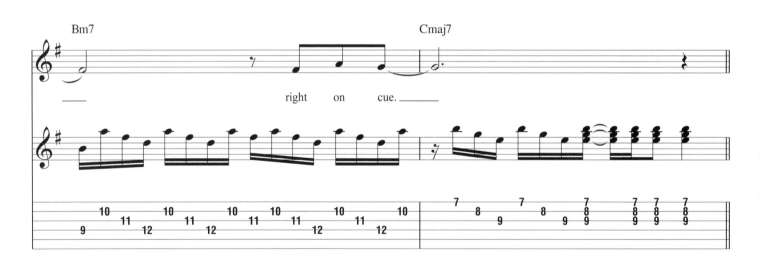

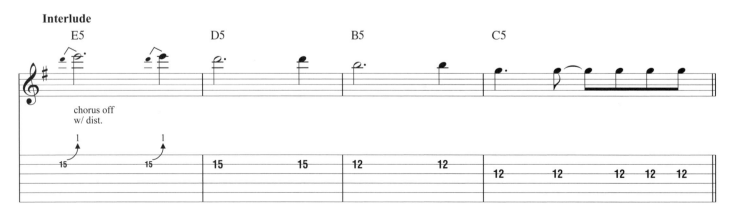

Verse

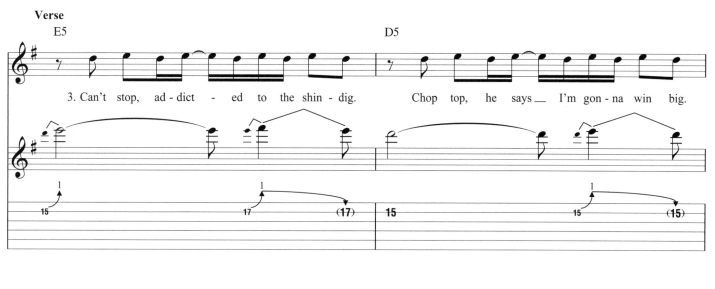

3. Can't stop, ad - dict - ed to the shin - dig. Chop top, he says __ I'm gon - na win big.

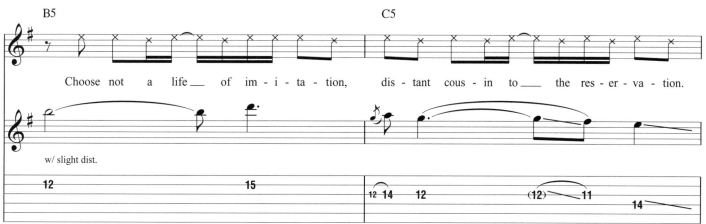

Choose not a life __ of im - i - ta - tion, dis - tant cous - in to __ the res - er - va - tion.

w/ slight dist.

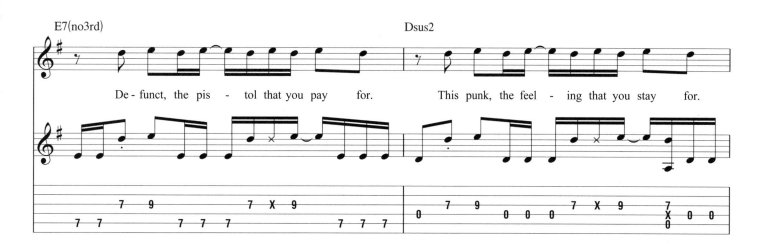

De - funct, the pis - tol that you pay for. This punk, the feel - ing that you stay for.

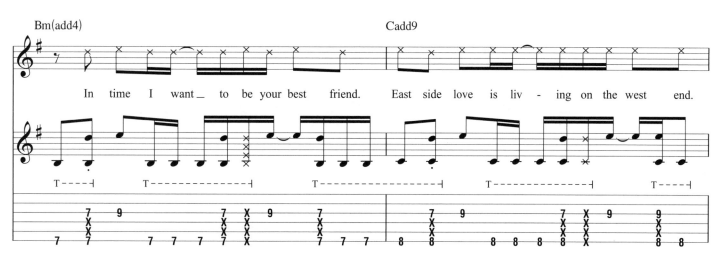

In time I want __ to be your best friend. East side love is liv - ing on the west end.

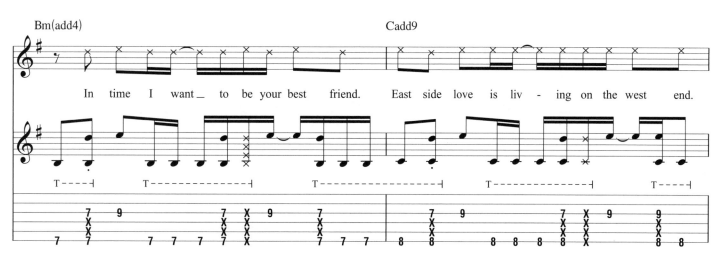

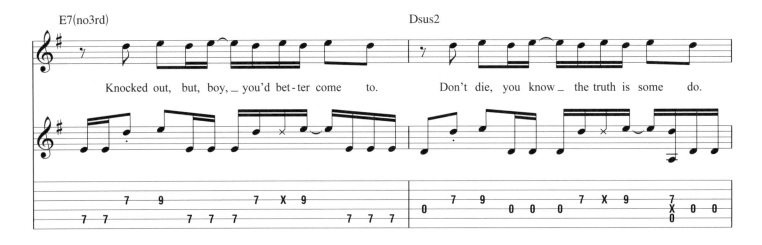

Knocked out, but, boy, _ you'd bet-ter come to. Don't die, you know _ the truth is some do.

Go write your mes - sage on the pave - ment. Burn-in' so bright, I won - der what the wave meant.

Kick start the gold - en gen-er - a - tor. Sweet-talk, but don't _ in-tim-i-date her.

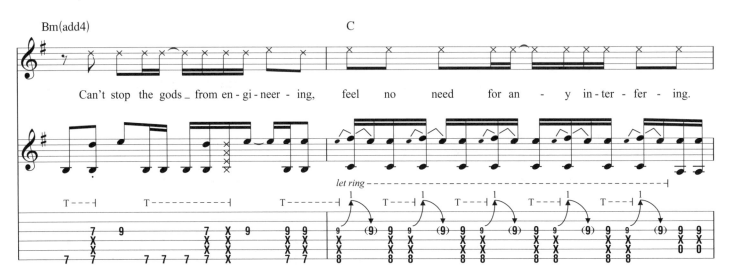

Can't stop the gods _ from en-gi-neer - ing, feel no need for an - y in-ter-fer - ing.

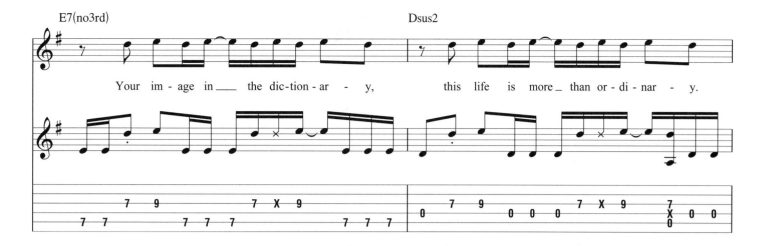

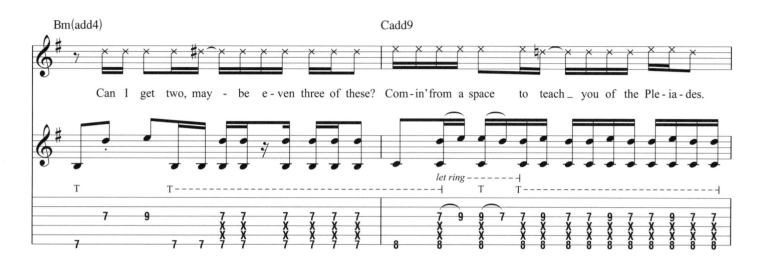

Additional Lyrics

2. Sweetheart is bleeding in the snow cone.
   So smart, she's leading me to ozone.
   Music, the great communicator,
   Use two sticks to make it in the nature.
   I'll get you into penetration,
   The gender of a generation.
   The birth of ev'ry other nation.
   Worth your weight, the gold of meditation.
   This chapter's gonna be a close one.
   Smoke rings, I know you're gonna blow one.
   All on a spaceship, persevering,
   Use my hands for ev'rything but steering.
   Can't stop the spirits when they need you.
   Moptops are happy when they feed you.
   J. Butterfly is in the treetop.
   Birds that blow the meaning into bebop.

Dani California

Words and Music by Anthony Kiedis, Flea, John Frusciante and Chad Smith

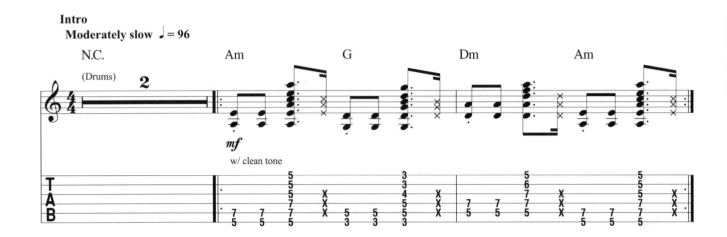

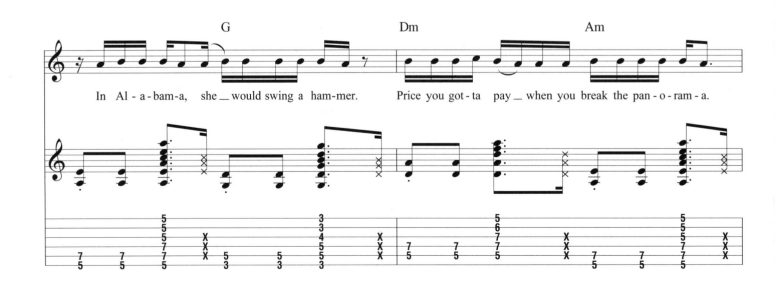

Outro-Guitar Solo

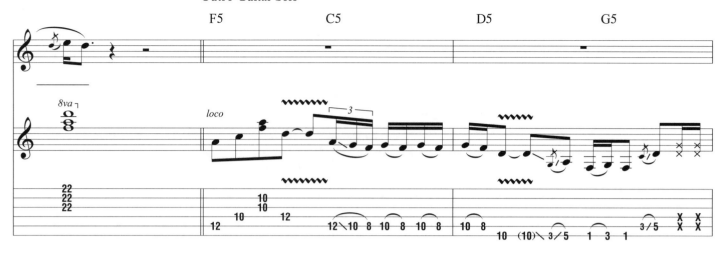

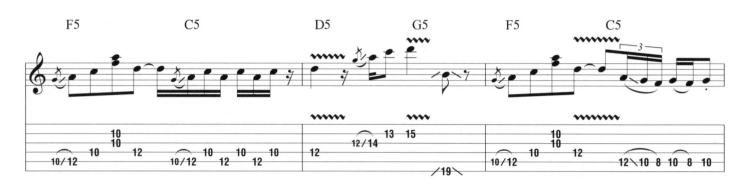

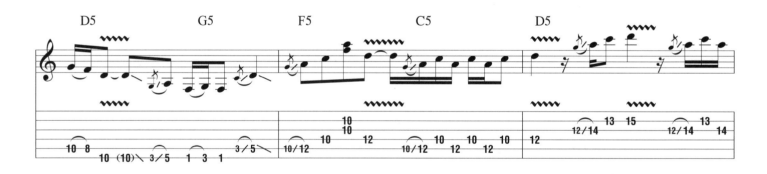

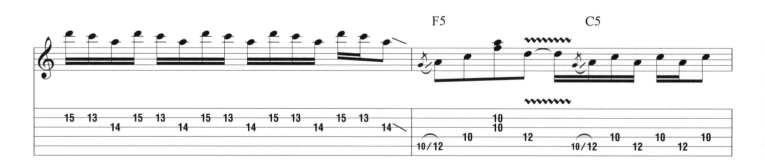

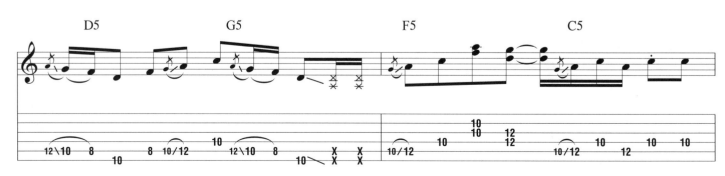

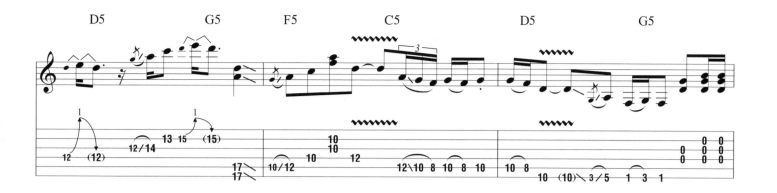

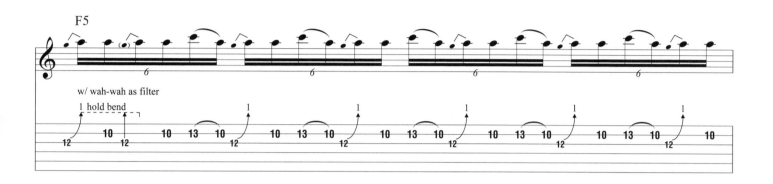

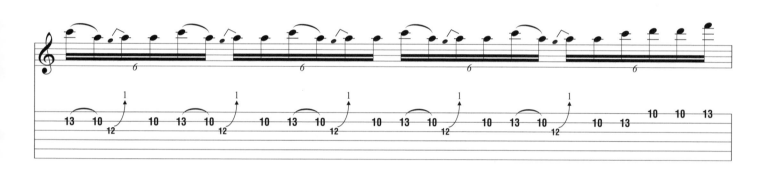

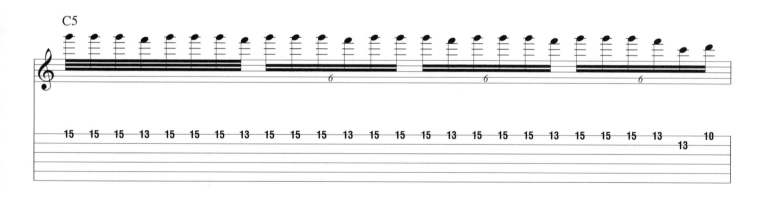

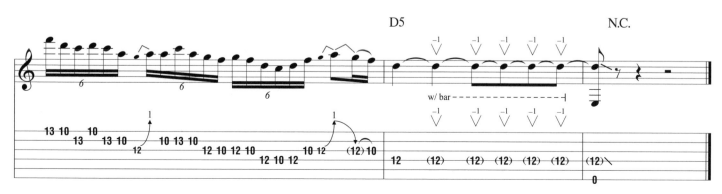

Dark Necessities

Words and Music by Anthony Kiedis, Flea, Chad Smith, Josh Klinghoffer and Brian Burton

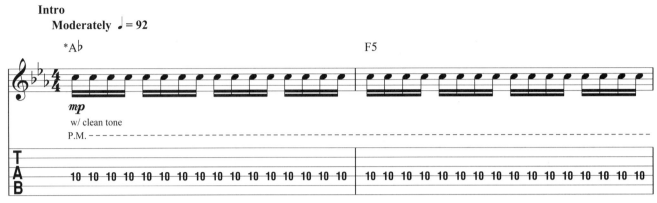

*Chord symbols reflect overall harmony.

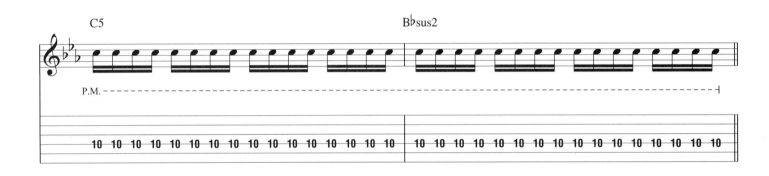

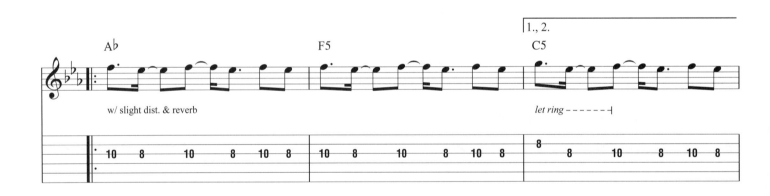

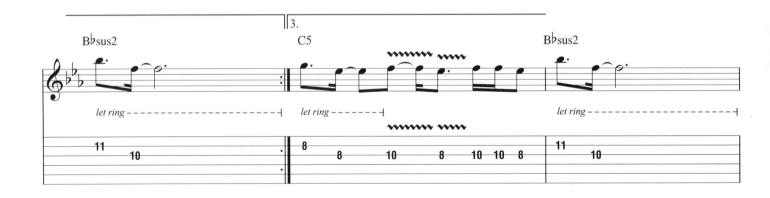

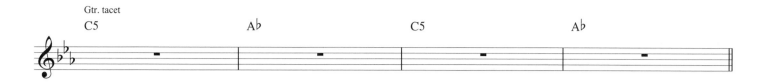

Gtr. tacet

Verse

1. Com-in' on to the light of day, _ we got man-y moons that are deep at play, _ so I

keep an eye on the shad-ow smile _ to see what it has to say. _____

Uh, you and I both know, uh, ev-'ry - thing _ must go a - way. _

Uh, what do you say?

mf
w/ wah
reverb off
*w/ slapback delay -------┤

6

*Set for 60 ms regeneration, 50% mix, feedback slightly above 100%.

𝄋 Verse

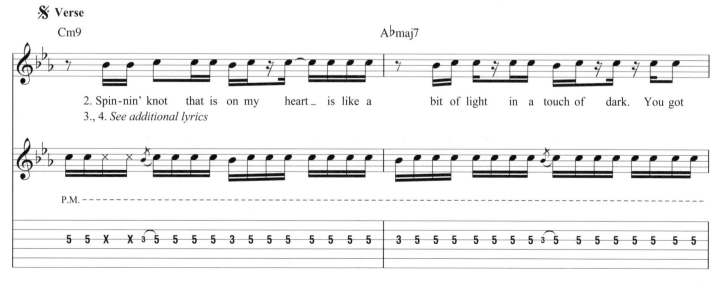

2. Spin-nin' knot that is on my heart _ is like a bit of light in a touch of dark. You got
3., 4. *See additional lyrics*

P.M. -

*Delay set for dotted eighth-note & quarter-note regeneration.

40

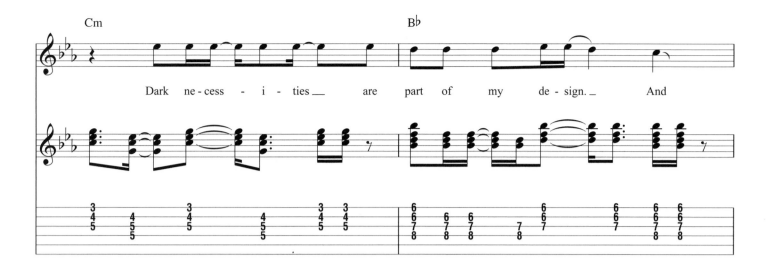

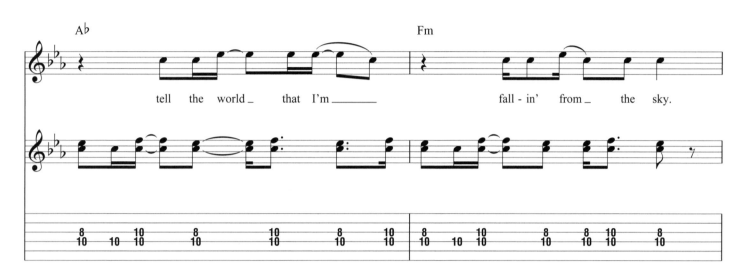

To Coda 1 ⊕   *To Coda 2* ⊕

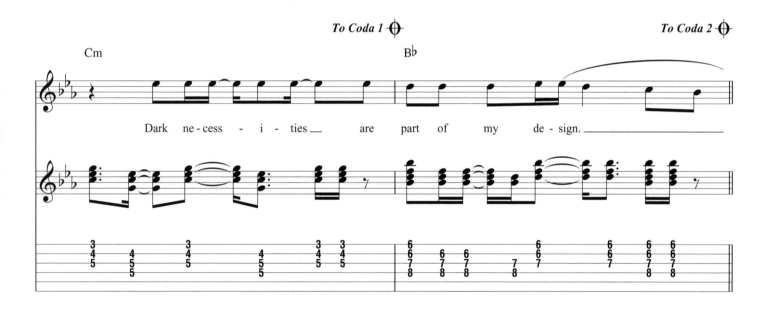

Interlude
*Gtr. tacet

*Delay off

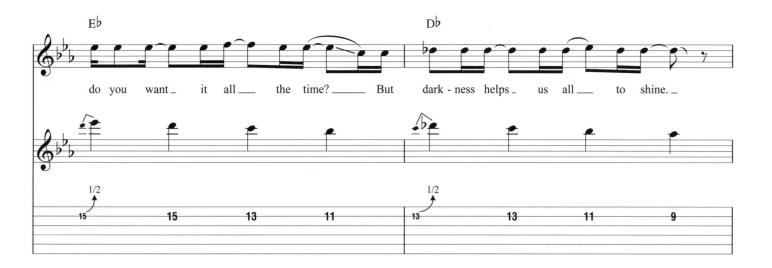

do you want _ it all _ the time? _____ But dark - ness helps _ us all _ to shine. _

D.S. al Coda 2

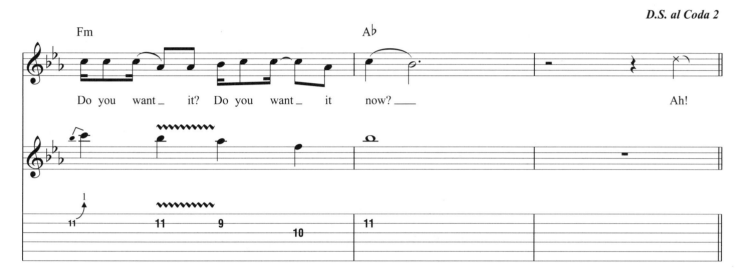

Do you want _ it? Do you want _ it now? _____ Ah!

Coda 2

Guitar Solo

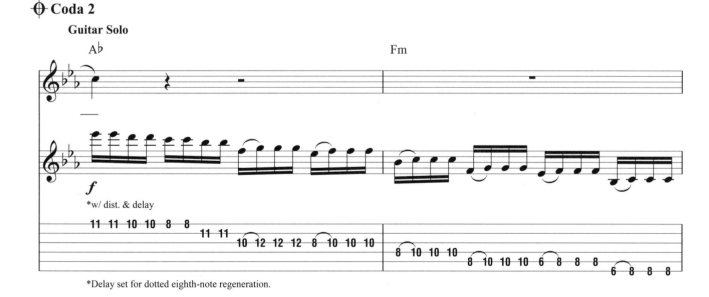

*w/ dist. & delay

*Delay set for dotted eighth-note regeneration.

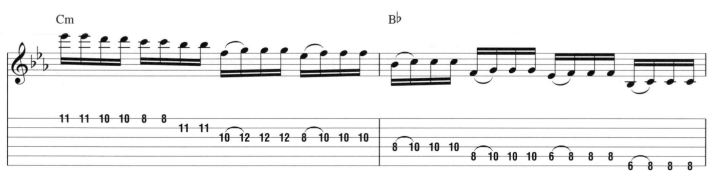

Additional Lyrics

3. Stumble down to the parkin' lot. You got no time for the afterthought.
   They're like ice cream for an astronaut. Well, that's me looking for we.
   Turn the corner and find the world at your command. Playin' the hand. Yeah!

4. Pick you up like a paperback with the track record of a maniac.
   So I move it in and, uh, we unpack. It's the same as yesterday.
   Any way we roll, ev'rything must go away. Uh, what do you say? Yeah!

Give It Away

Words and Music by Anthony Kiedis, Flea, John Frusciante and Chad Smith

Intro
Moderate Funk ♩ = 92

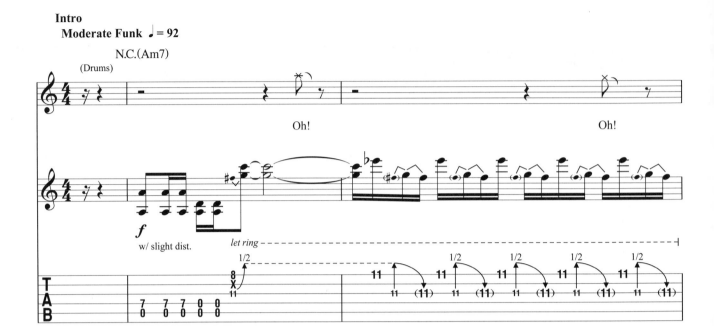

Oh!   Oh!

𝄋 Verse

N.C.(Am7)

1., 4. What I've got, you've got to give it to your mam - ma.   What I've got, you've got to give it to your pa - pa.
2., 3. *See additional lyrics*

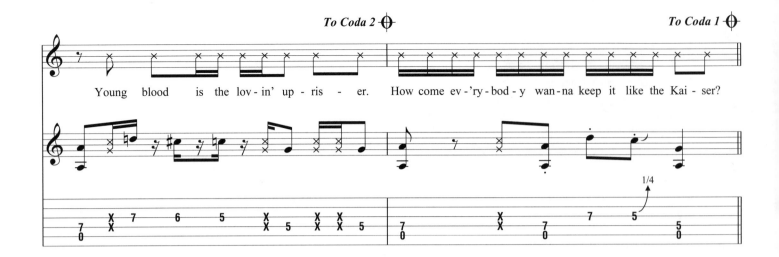

Young blood is the lov-in' up-ris - er. How come ev-'ry-bod-y wan-na keep it like the Kai-ser?

Chorus

N.C.(A5)

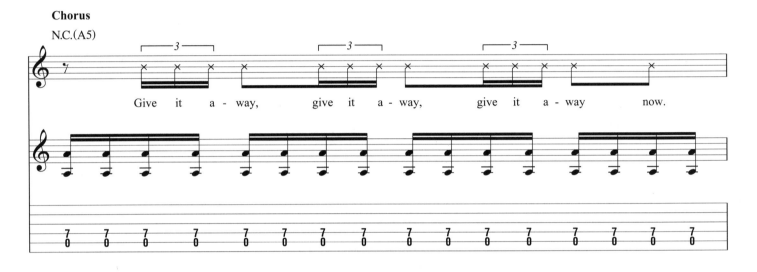

Give it a - way, give it a - way, give it a - way now.

2nd time, substitute Fill 1

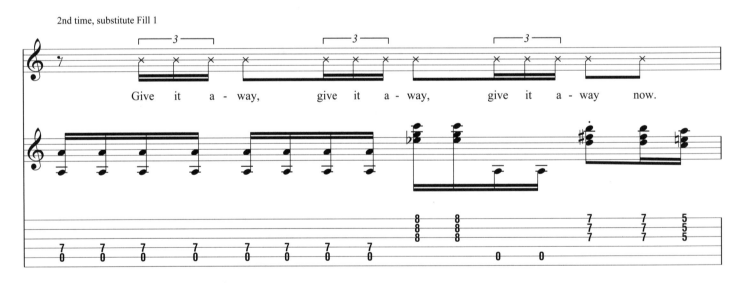

Give it a - way, give it a - way, give it a - way now.

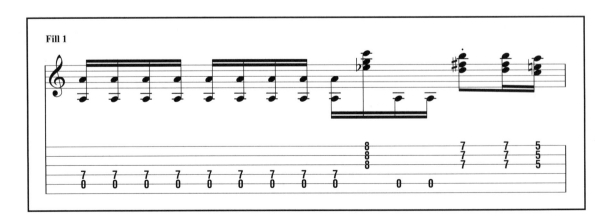

Fill 1

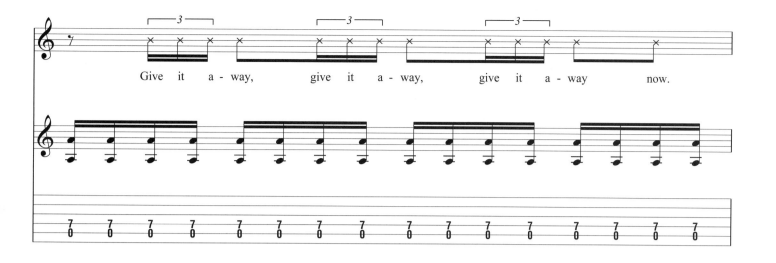

Give it a - way, give it a - way, give it a - way now.

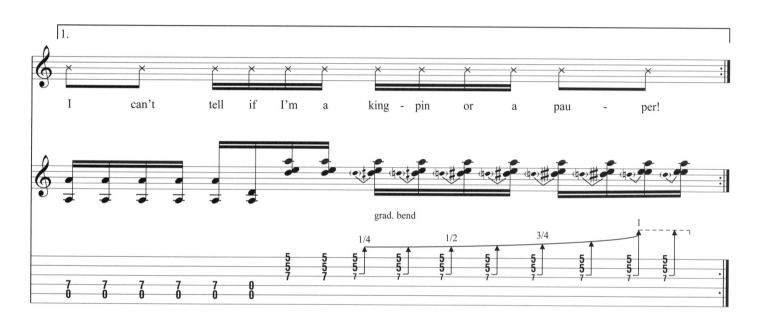

1.

I can't tell if I'm a king - pin or a pau - per!

grad. bend

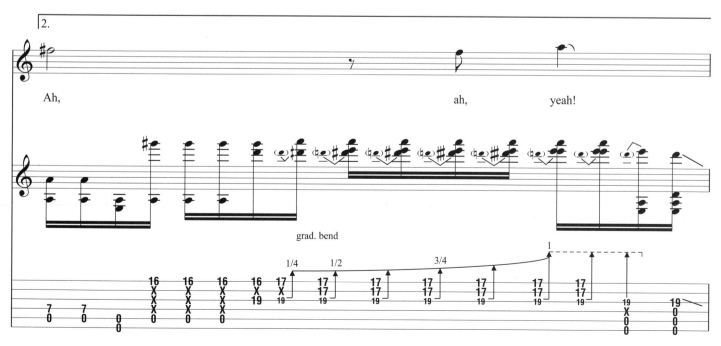

2.

Ah, ah, yeah!

grad. bend

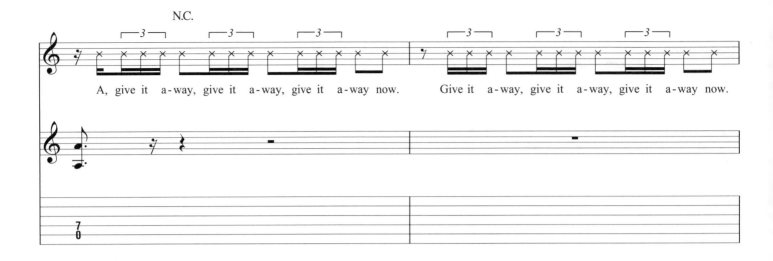

A, give it a-way, give it a-way, give it a-way now. Give it a-way, give it a-way, give it a-way now.

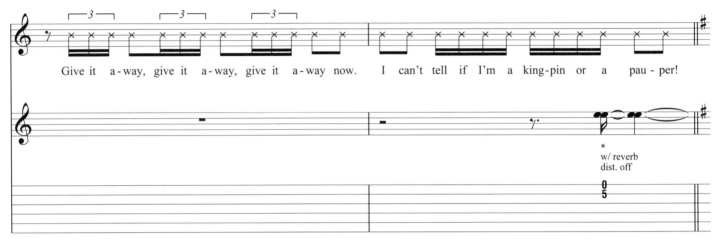

Give it a-way, give it a-way, give it a-way now. I can't tell if I'm a king-pin or a pau-per!

*
w/ reverb
dist. off

*Backwards gtr., next 8 meas.

Guitar Solo

N.C.(Em)

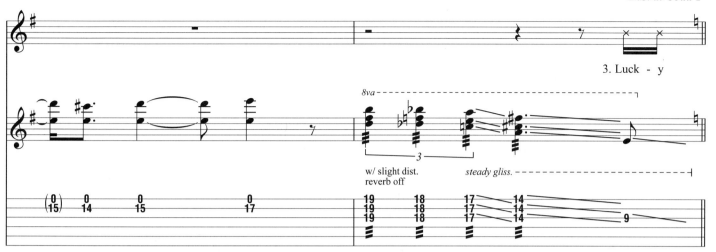

3. Luck - y

⊕ Coda 1
Chorus

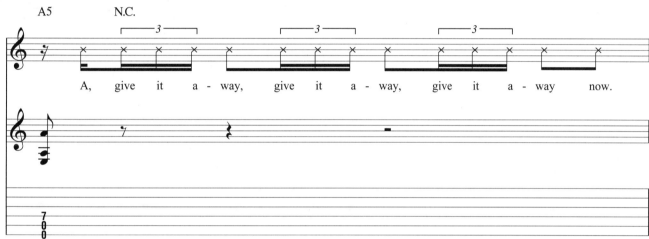

A, give it a-way, give it a-way, give it a-way now.

Gtr. tacet

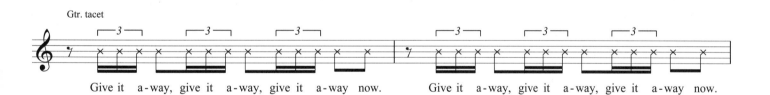

Give it a-way, give it a-way, give it a-way now. Give it a-way, give it a-way, give it a-way now.

Guitar Solo

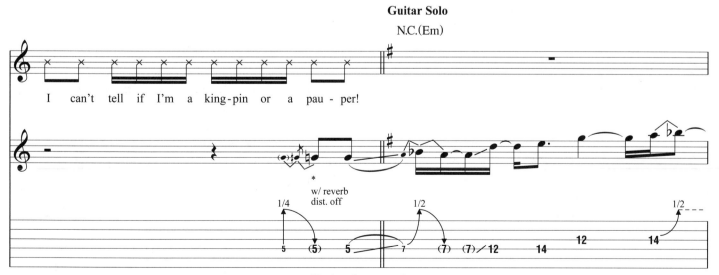

I can't tell if I'm a king-pin or a pau-per!

*Backwards gtr., next 5 meas.

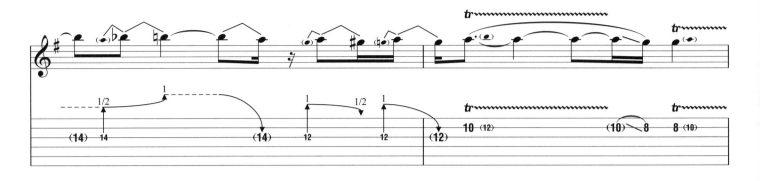

D.S. al Coda 2

⊕ Coda 2

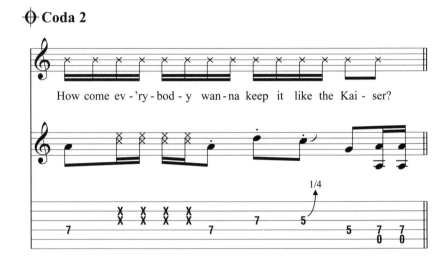

How come ev-'ry-bod-y wan-na keep it like the Kai - ser?

Outro-Chorus

N.C.(A5)

Give it a-way, give it a-way, give it a-way now. Give it a-way, give it a-way, give it a-way now.

Give it a-way, give it a-way, give it a-way now. Give it a-way, give it a-way, give it a-way now.

Additional Lyrics

2. Greedy little people in a sea of distress,
   Keep your more to receive your less.
   Unimpressed by material excess.
   Love is free, love me, say hell yes.
   I'm a lowbrow but I rock a little know-how.
   No time for the piggies or the hoosegow.
   Get smart, get down with the powwow.
   Never been a better time than right now.
   Bob Marley, poet and a prophet.
   Bob Marley taught me how to off it.
   Bob Marley walkin' like he talk it.
   Goodness me, can't you see I'm gonna cough it?

3. Lucky me, swimmin' in my ability,
   Dancin' down on life with agility.
   Come and drink it up from my fertility,
   Blessed with a bucket of lucky mobility.
   My mom, I love her 'cause she love me.
   Long gone are the times when she scrub me.
   Feelin' good, my brother gonna hug me.
   Drink my juice, young love chug-a-lug me.
   There's a river born to be a giver,
   Keep you warm, won't let you shiver.
   His heart is never gonna wither.
   Come on ev'rybody, time to deliver.

My Friends

Words and Music by Anthony Kiedis, Flea, Chad Smith and David Navarro

Drop D tuning:
(low to high) D-A-D-G-B-E

Intro

Moderately ♩ = 82

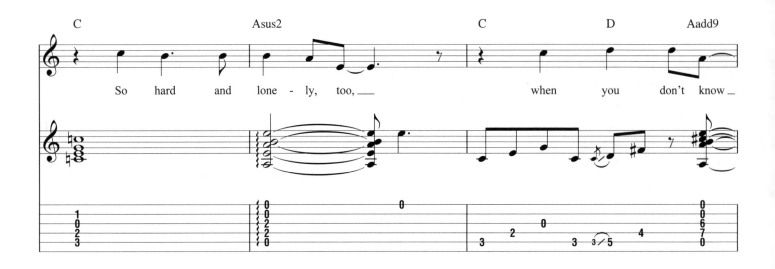

So hard and lone - ly, too, ___ when you don't know ___

Guitar Solo

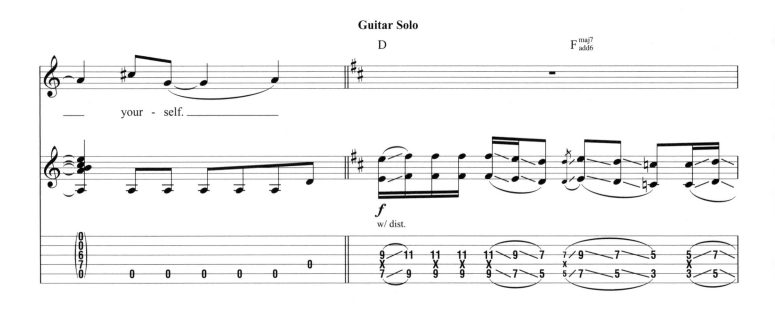

___ your - self. ___

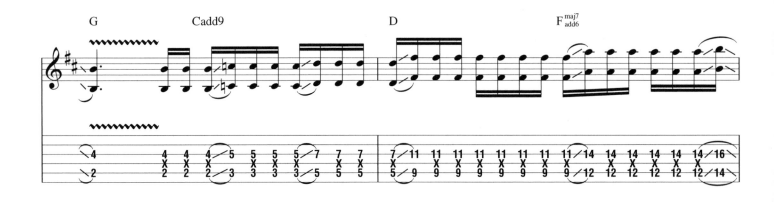

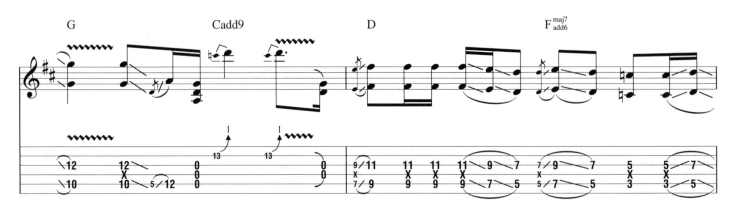

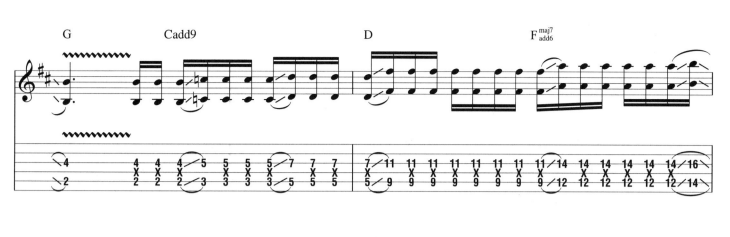

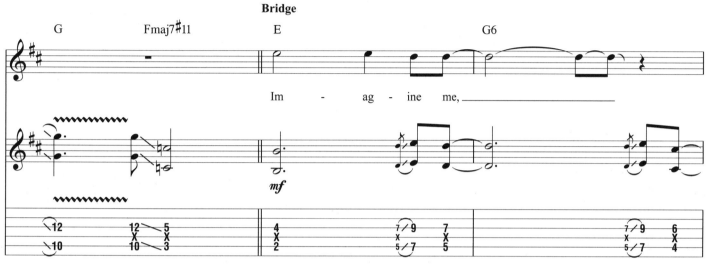

Bridge

Im - ag - ine me, _____

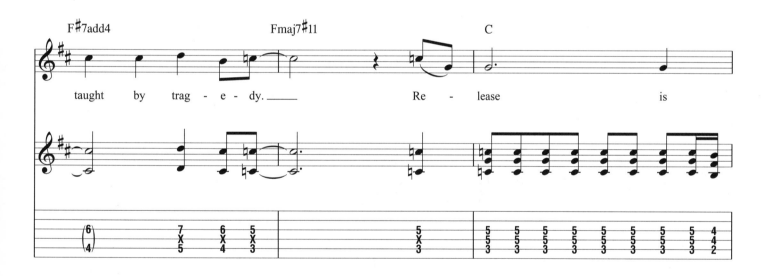

taught by trag - e - dy. _____ Re - lease is

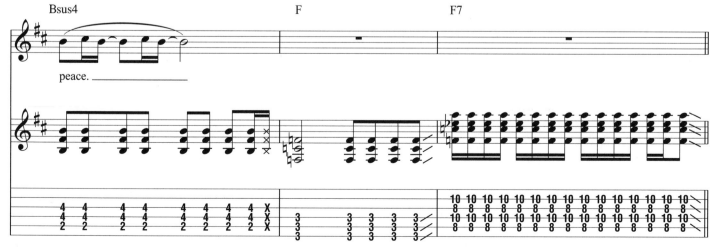

peace.

Otherside

Words and Music by Anthony Kiedis, Flea, John Frusciante and Chad Smith

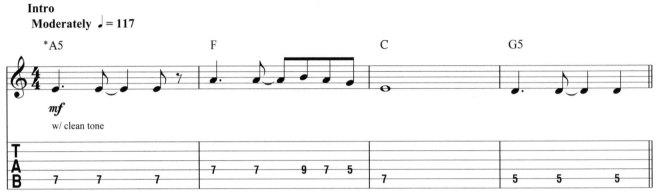

*Chord symbols reflect overall harmony.

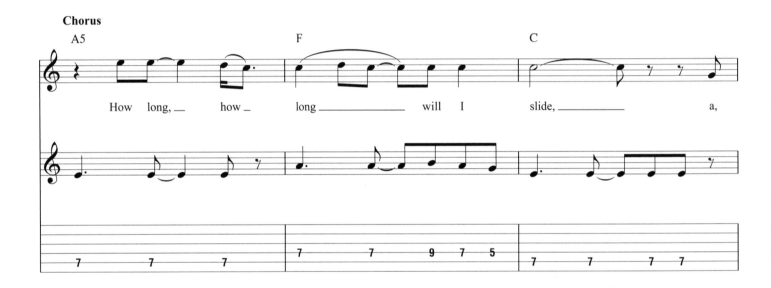

How long, — how — long _____ will I slide, _____ a,

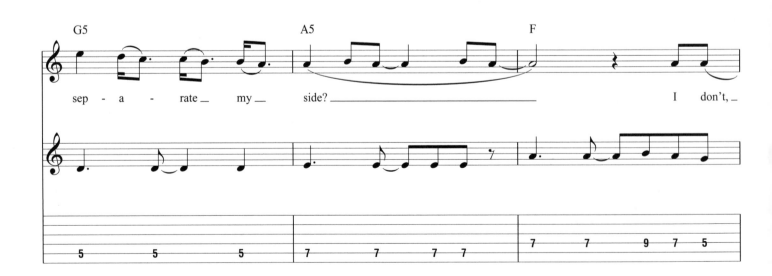

sep - a - rate — my — side? _____ I don't, —

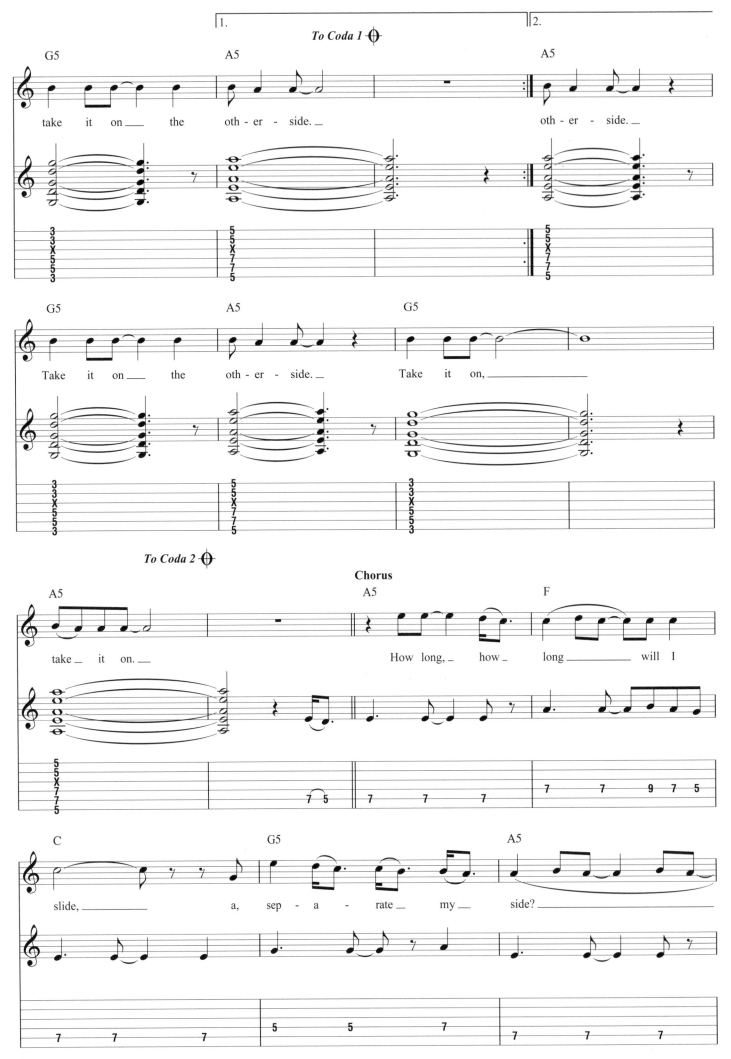

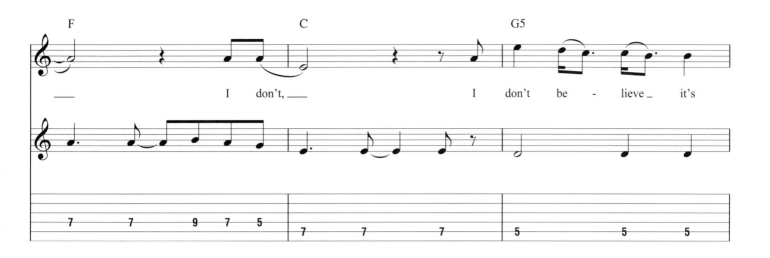

D.S. al Coda 1
(take 1st ending)

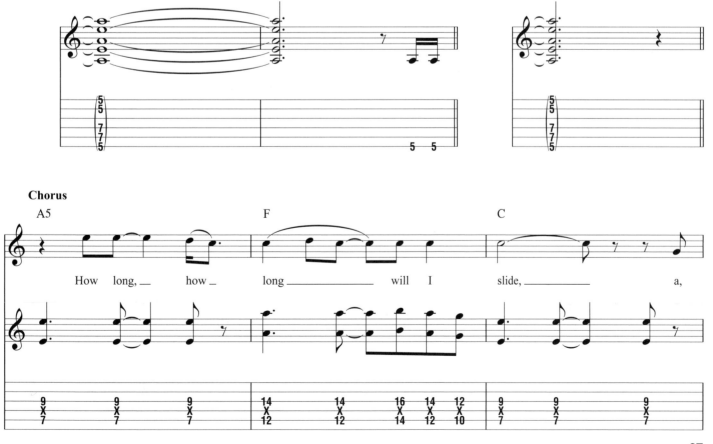

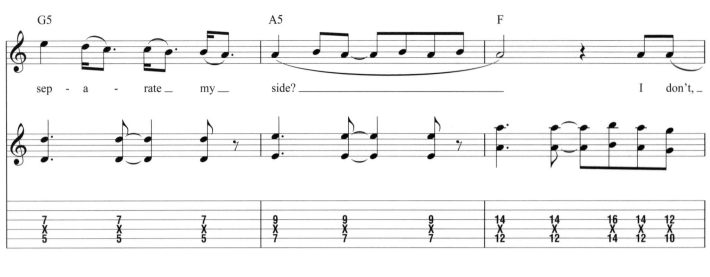

sep - a - rate _ my _ side? _____ I don't, _

_ I don't be - lieve _ it's bad. _____

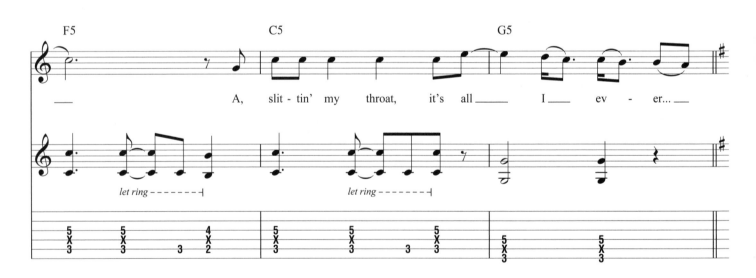

_ A, slit - tin' my throat, it's all _____ I ___ ev - er... ___

Bridge
Slightly faster ♩ = 128

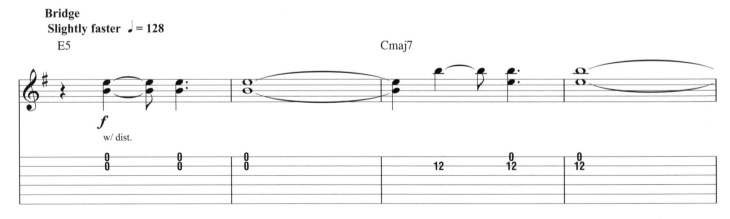

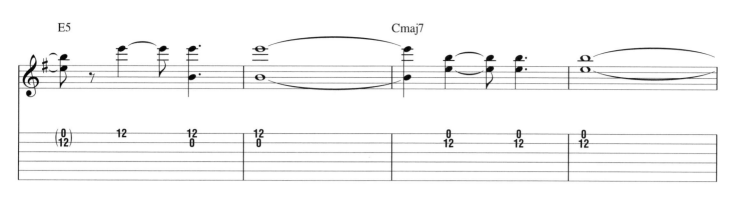

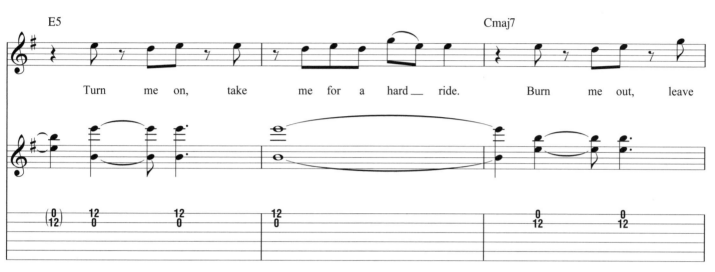

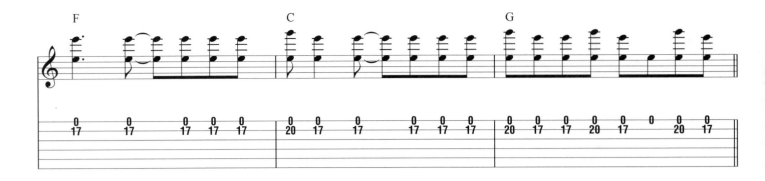

Outro-Chorus

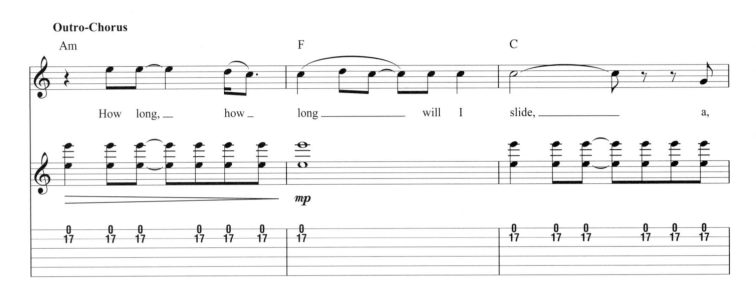

How long, — how long will I slide, — a,

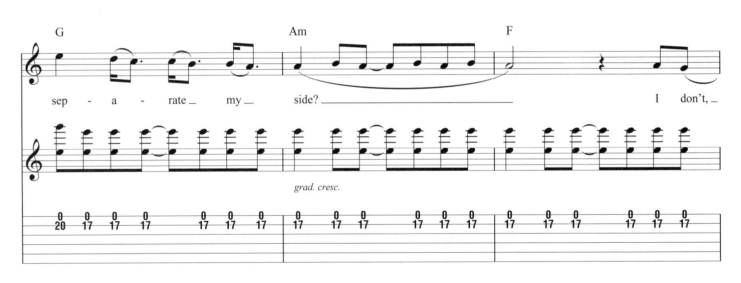

sep - a - rate my side? I don't,

I don't be - lieve it's bad.

Additional Lyrics

2. Centuries are what it meant to me,
   A cemetery where I marry the sea.
   Stranger things could never change my mind.
   I got to take it on the otherside.
   Take it on the otherside. Take it on, take it on.

3. Pour my life into a paper cup.
   The ashtray's full and I'm spillin' my guts.
   She wants to know, am I still a slut.
   I got to take it on the otherside.

4. Scarlet starlet and she's in my bed,
   A candidate, a, for my soul mate bled.
   Push the trigger and pull the thread.
   I got to take it on the otherside.
   Take it on the otherside. Take it on, take it on.

Road Trippin'

Words and Music by Anthony Kiedis, Flea, John Frusciante and Chad Smith

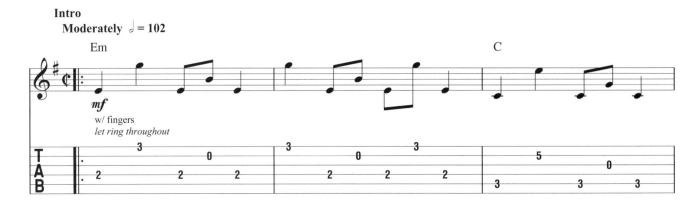

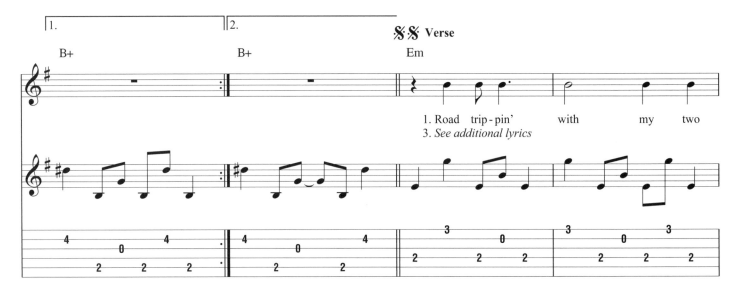

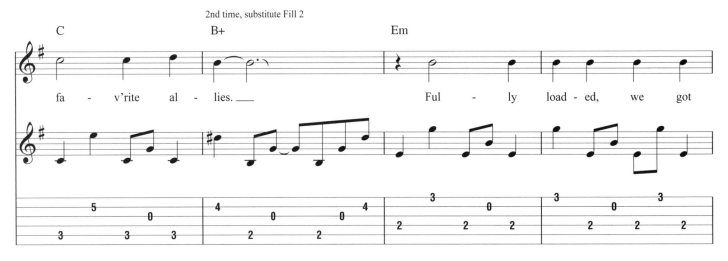

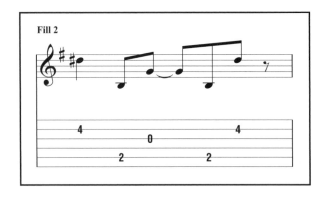

snacks and sup - plies. _____ It's time to leave __ this town, it's

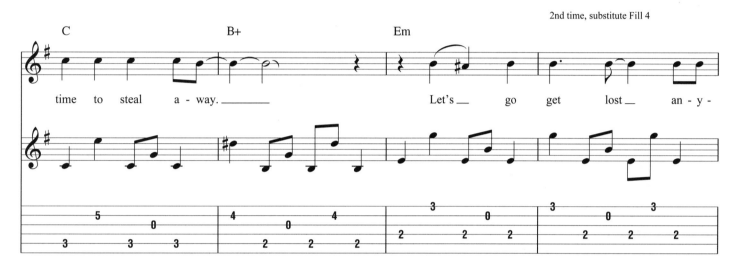

time to steal a - way. _____ Let's __ go get lost __ an - y -

where in the U. S. A. ___ Let's go get lost, __ let's go get lost. _

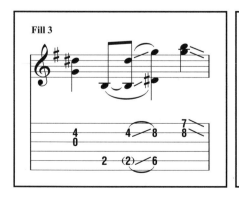

Fill 3

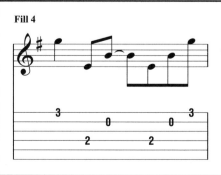

Fill 4

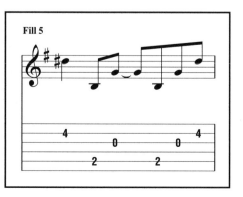

Fill 5

2nd time, substitute Fill 1

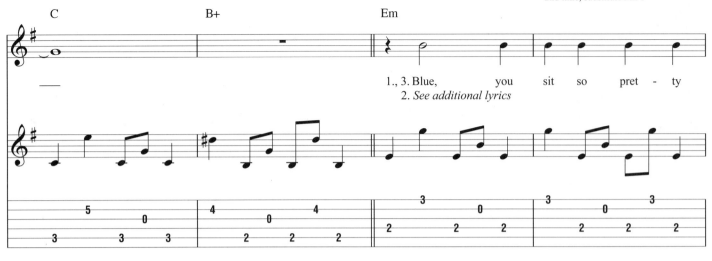

1., 3. Blue,   you   sit so   pret - ty
2. *See additional lyrics*

3rd time, substitute Fill 4

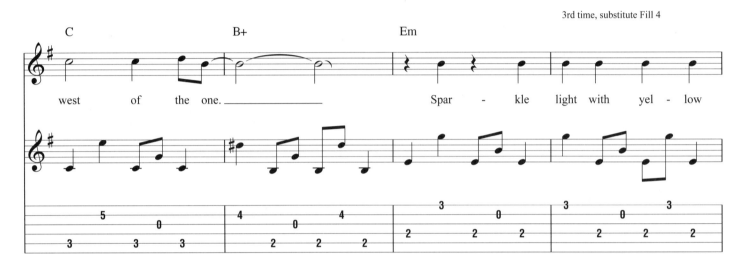

west   of the one. _____   Spar - kle   light with   yel - low

3rd time, substitute Fill 5

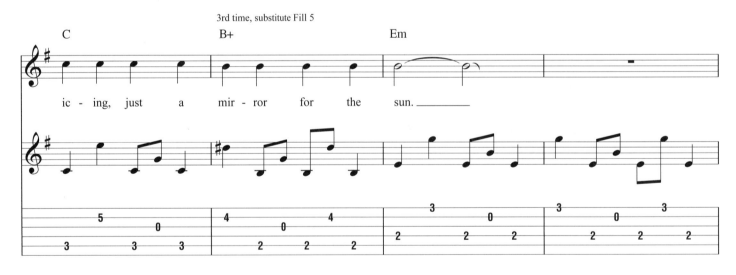

ic - ing, just   a   mir - ror   for   the   sun. _____

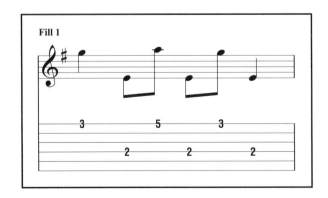

Fill 1

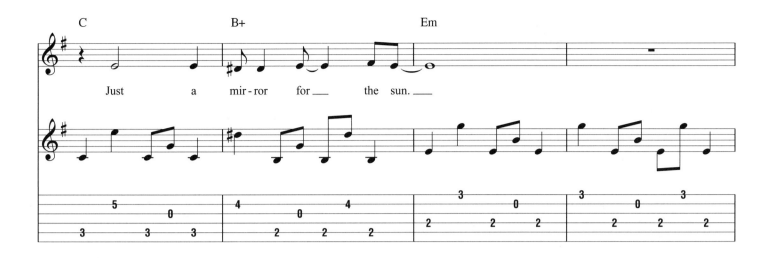

Just a mir-ror for ___ the sun. ___

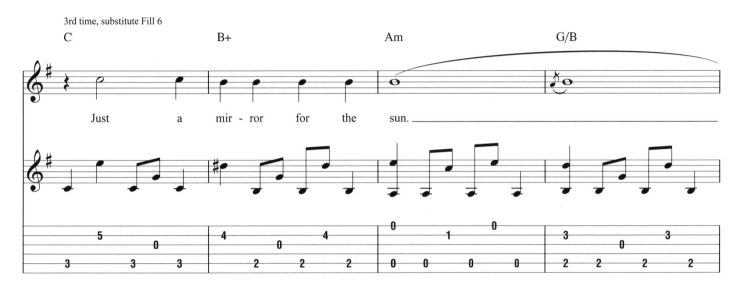

3rd time, substitute Fill 6

Just a mir - ror for the sun. ___

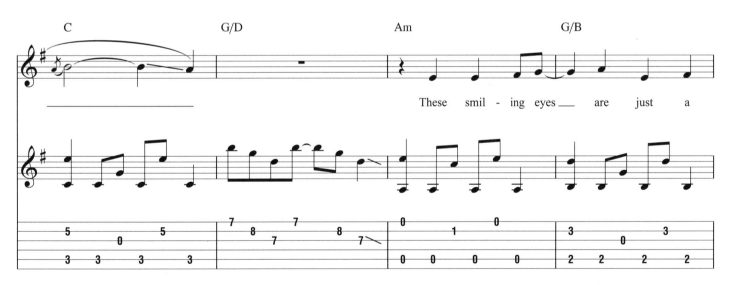

___

These smil - ing eyes ___ are just a

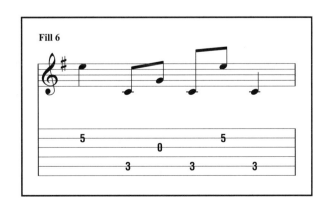

Fill 6

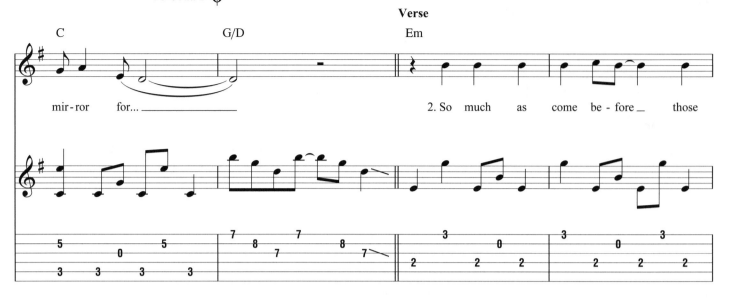

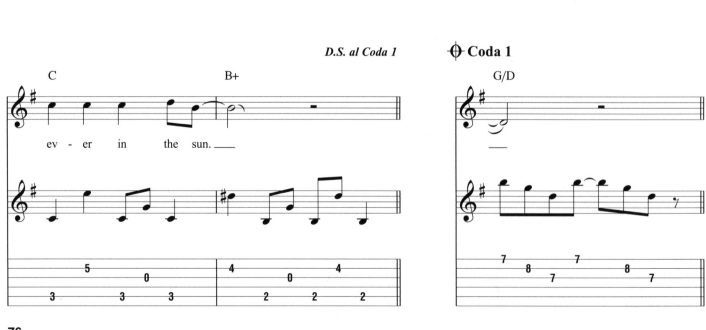

Interlude

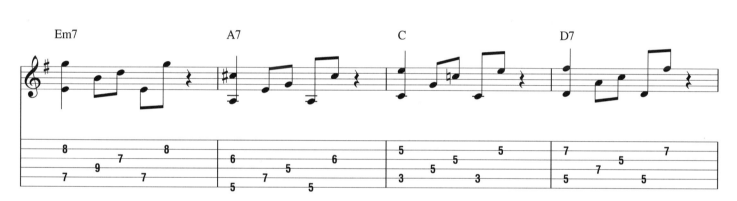

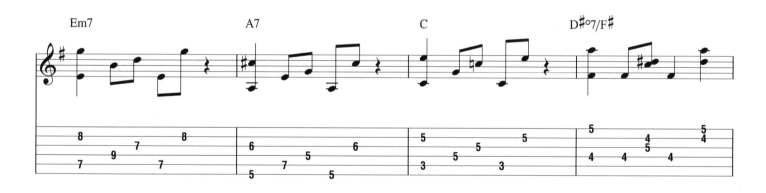

D.S.S. al Coda 2

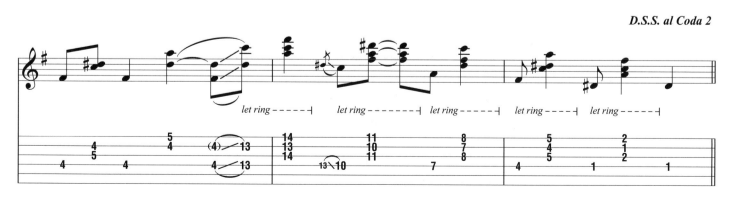

⊕ Coda 2

Outro

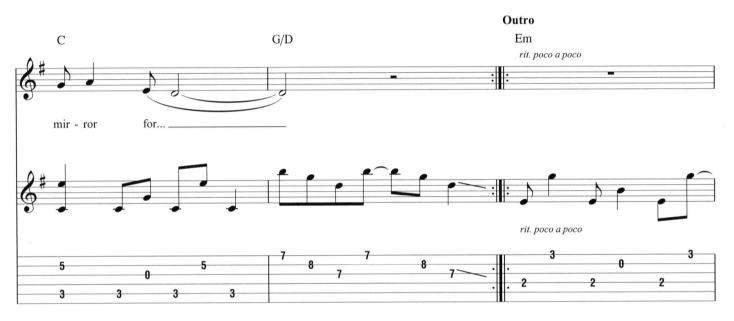

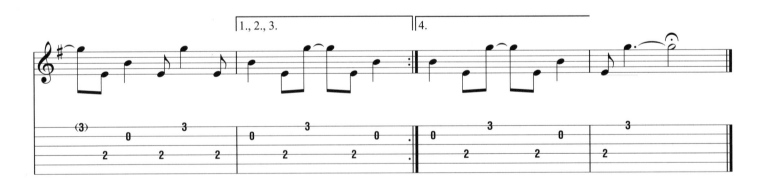

Additional Lyrics

Chorus 2. Now let us check our heads and let us check the surf.
Staying high and dry's more trouble than it's worth in the sun.
Just a mirror for the sun.
Just a mirror for the sun.
These smiling eyes are just a mirror for...

3. In Big Sur we take some time to linger on.
We three hunky dory's got our snakefinger on.
Now let us drink the stars; it's time to steal away.
Let's go get lost right here in the U. S. A.
Let's go get lost, let's go get lost.

Suck My Kiss

Words and Music by Anthony Kiedis, Flea, John Frusciante and Chad Smith

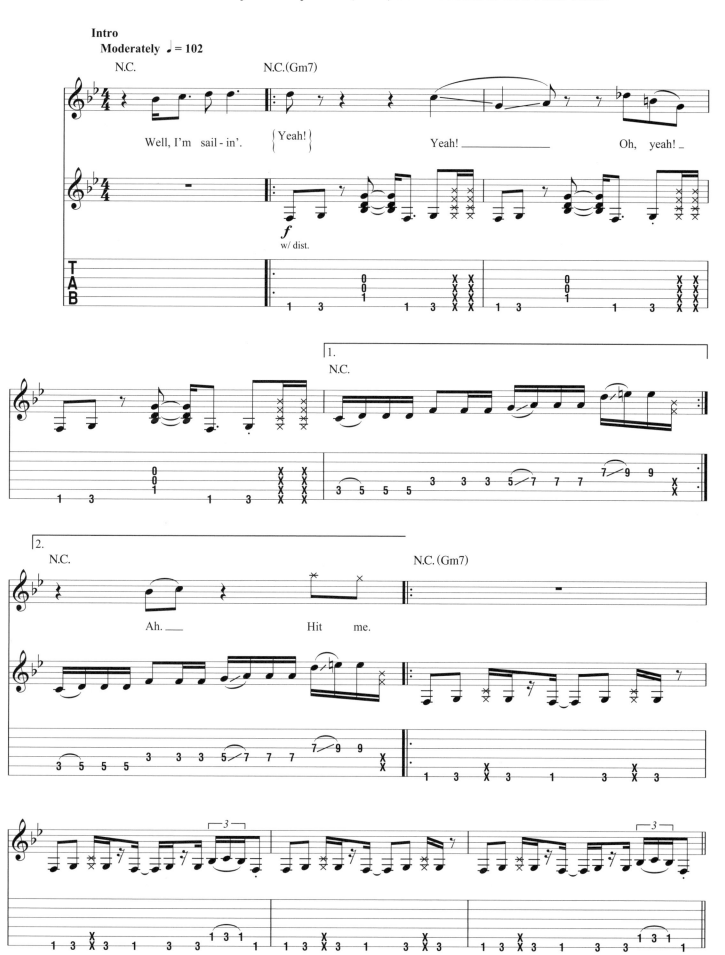

Give to me sweet sacred bliss.

mouth was made to suck my kiss!

mouth was made to.

2nd time, substitute Fill 1

Guitar Solo

N.C.(Gm7)

N.C.

Fill 1

82

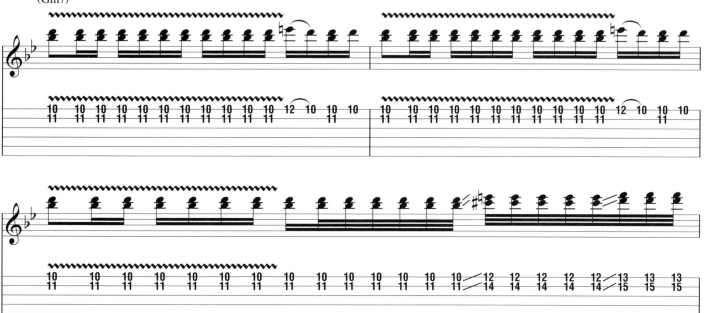

D.S. al Coda

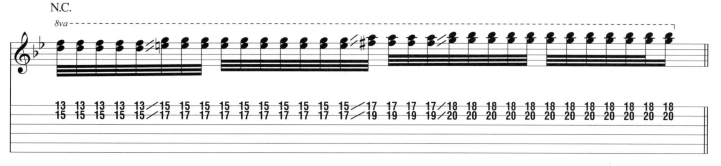

Give to me __ sweet sa - cred bliss. That mouth was made to suck my kiss!

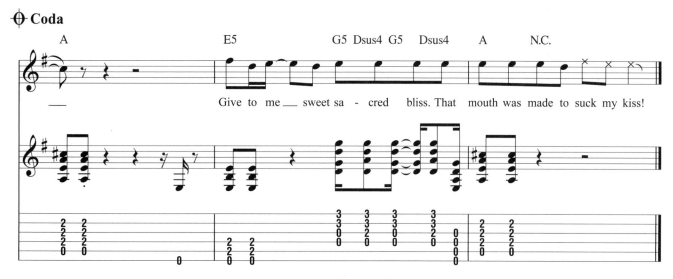

Additional Lyrics

2. Look at me; can't you see?
All I really want to be
Is free from a world that hurts me.
I need relief.
Do you want me, girl, to be your thief?
Aw, baby, just for you
I'd steal anything that you want me to.
K-I-S-S-I-N-G,
Chick a chick a dee, do me like a banshee.
Low brow is how,
Swimmin' in the sound of a bow wow wow.
Aw, baby, do me now.
Do me here, I do allow.

Scar Tissue

Words and Music by Anthony Kiedis, Flea, John Frusciante and Chad Smith

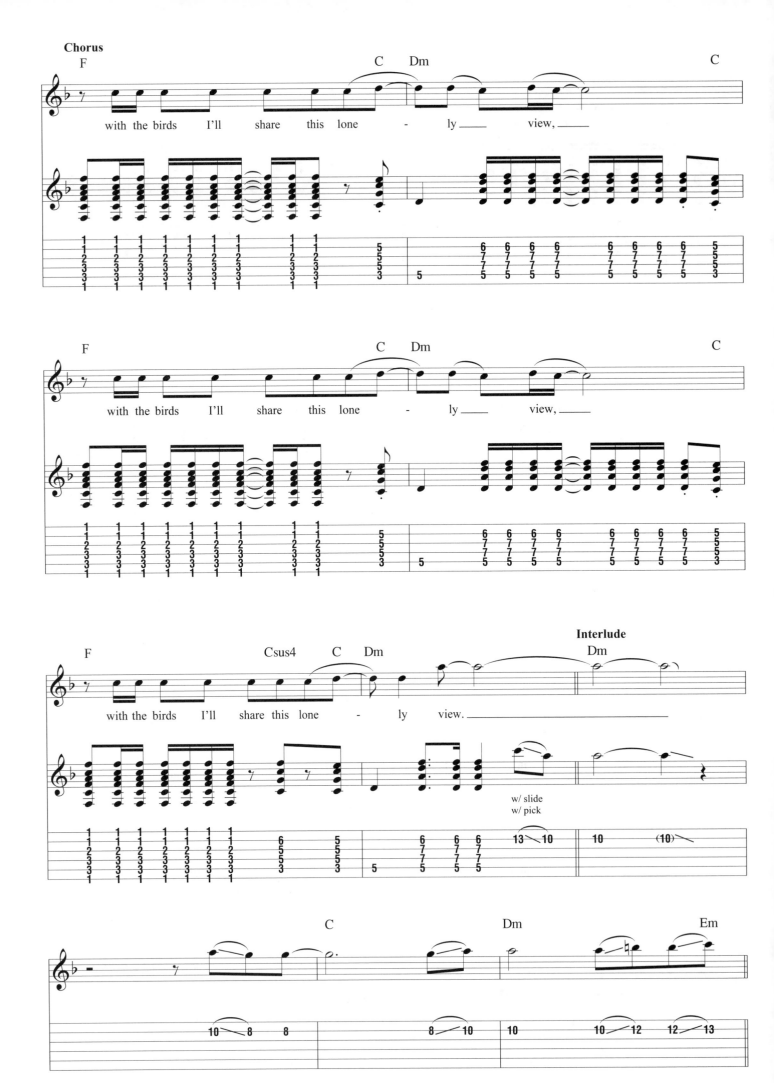

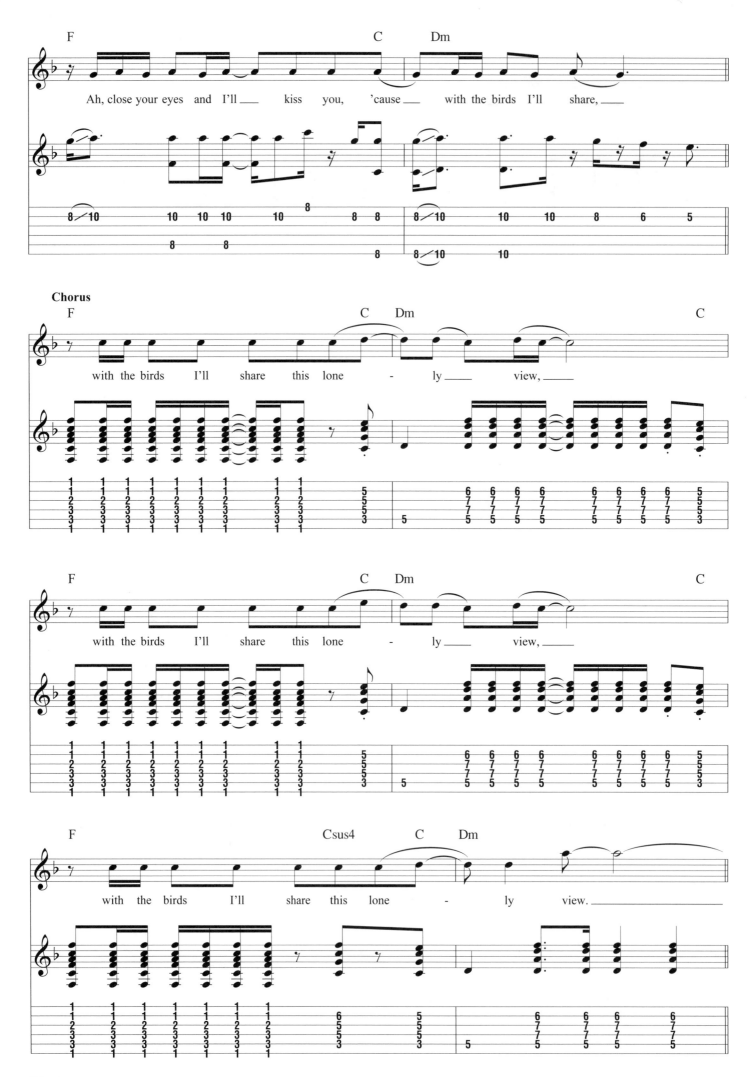

Chorus

Outro-Guitar Solo

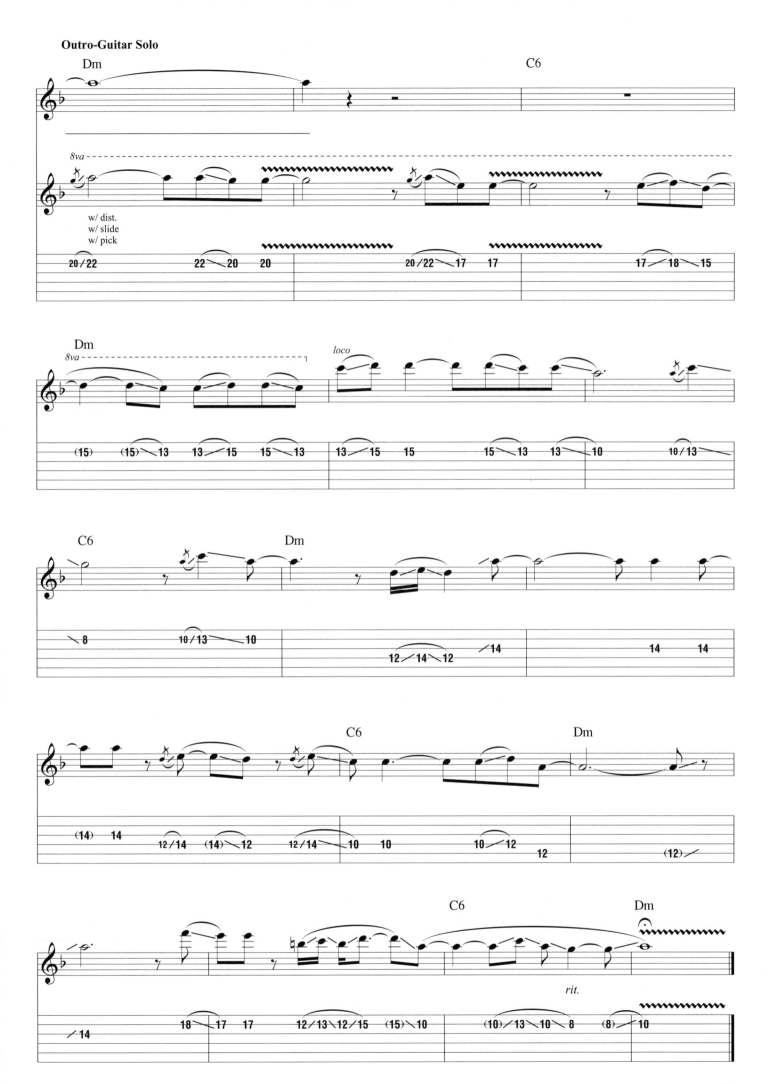

Snow (Hey Oh)

Words and Music by Anthony Kiedis, Flea, John Frusciante and Chad Smith

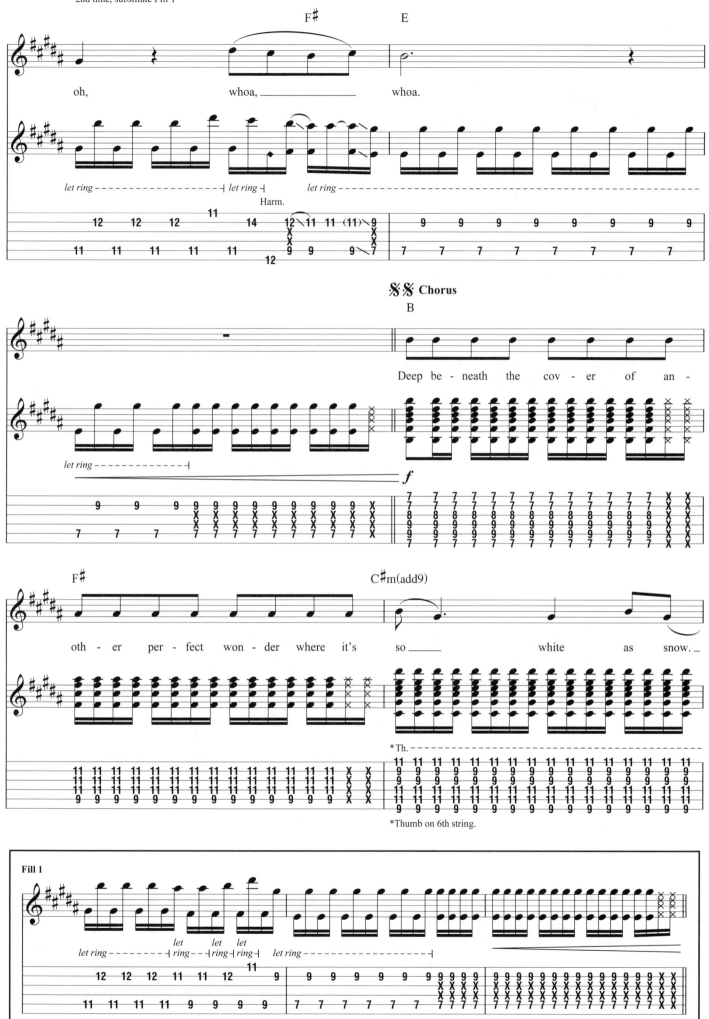

2nd time, substitute Fill 1

§ § Chorus

*Thumb on 6th string.

Fill 1

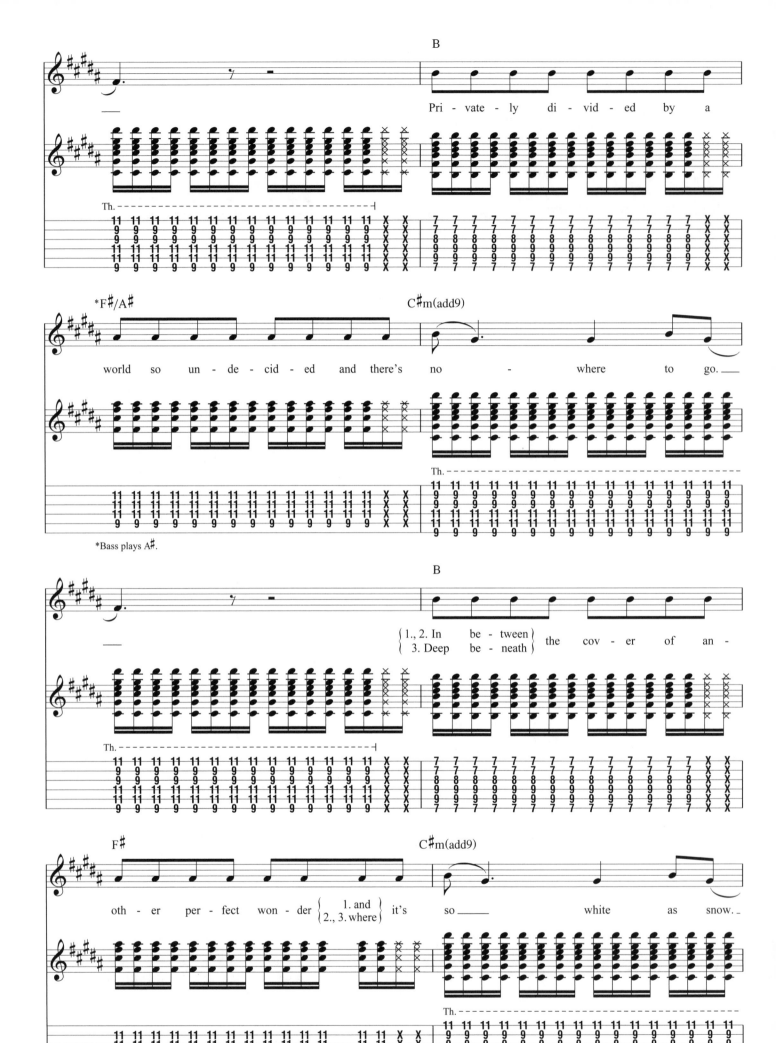

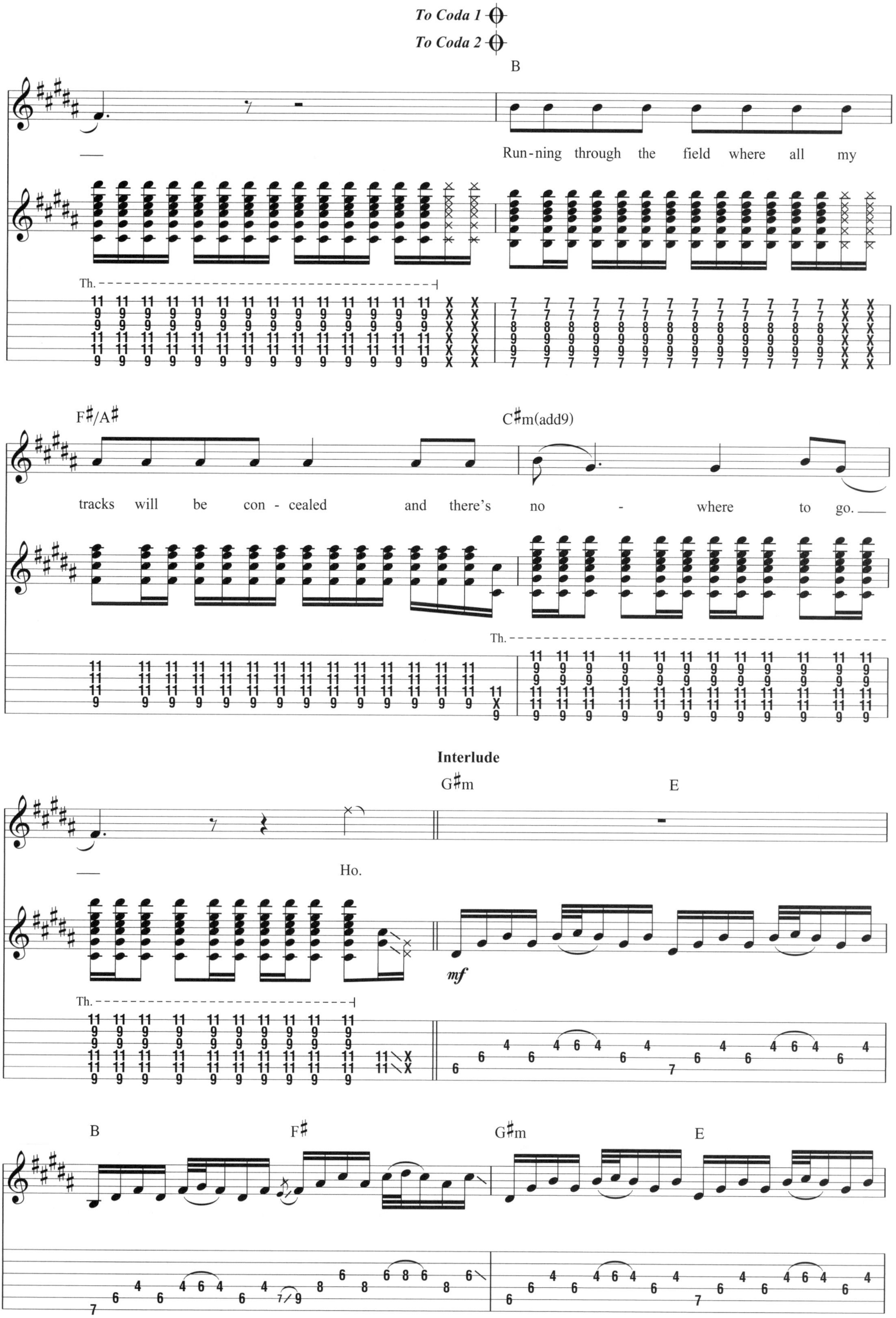
To Coda 1
To Coda 2
B
Run-ning through the field where all my
Th.
F♯/A♯
C♯m(add9)
tracks will be con - cealed and there's no - where to go.
Th.
Interlude
G♯m
E
Ho.
mf
Th.
B
F♯
G♯m
E

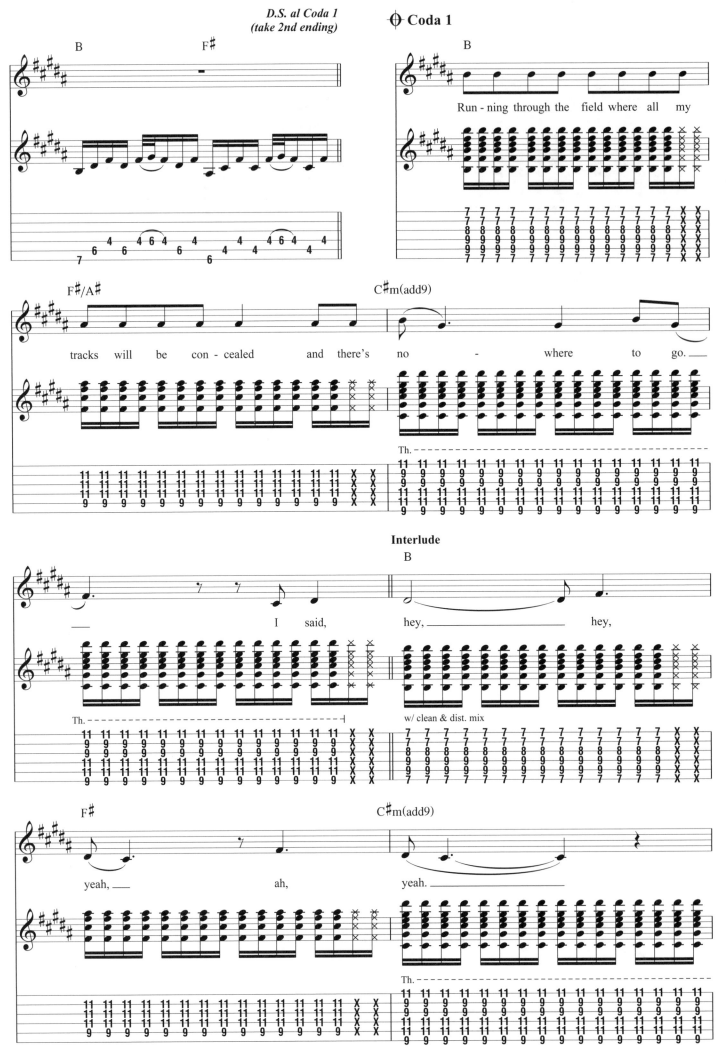

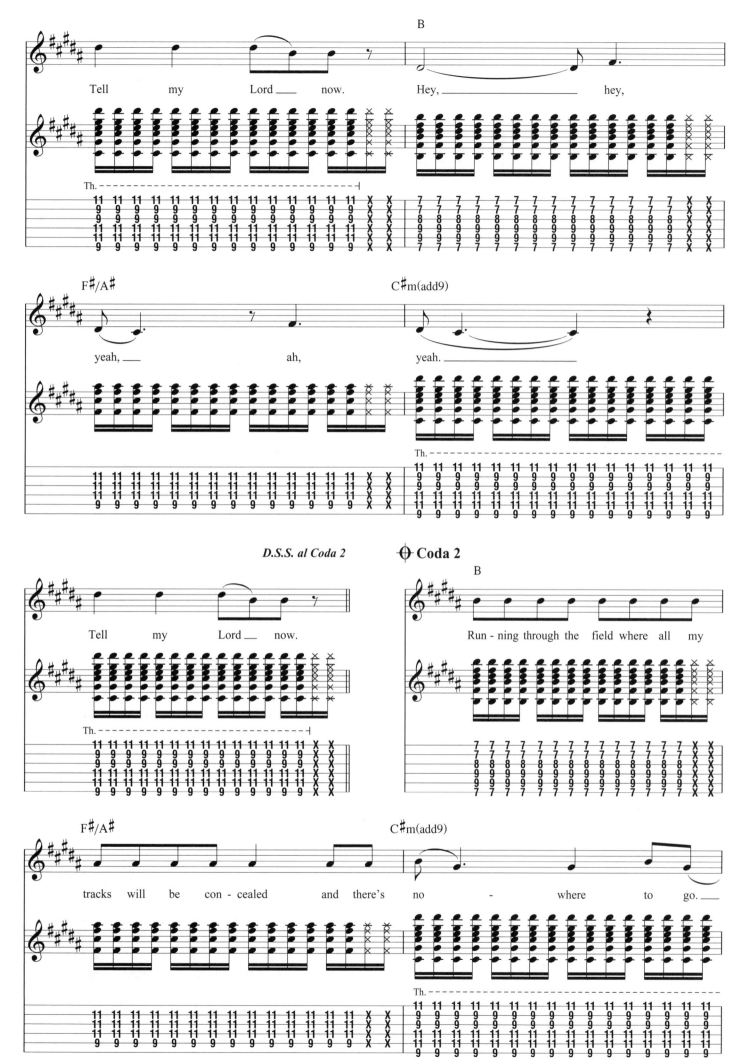

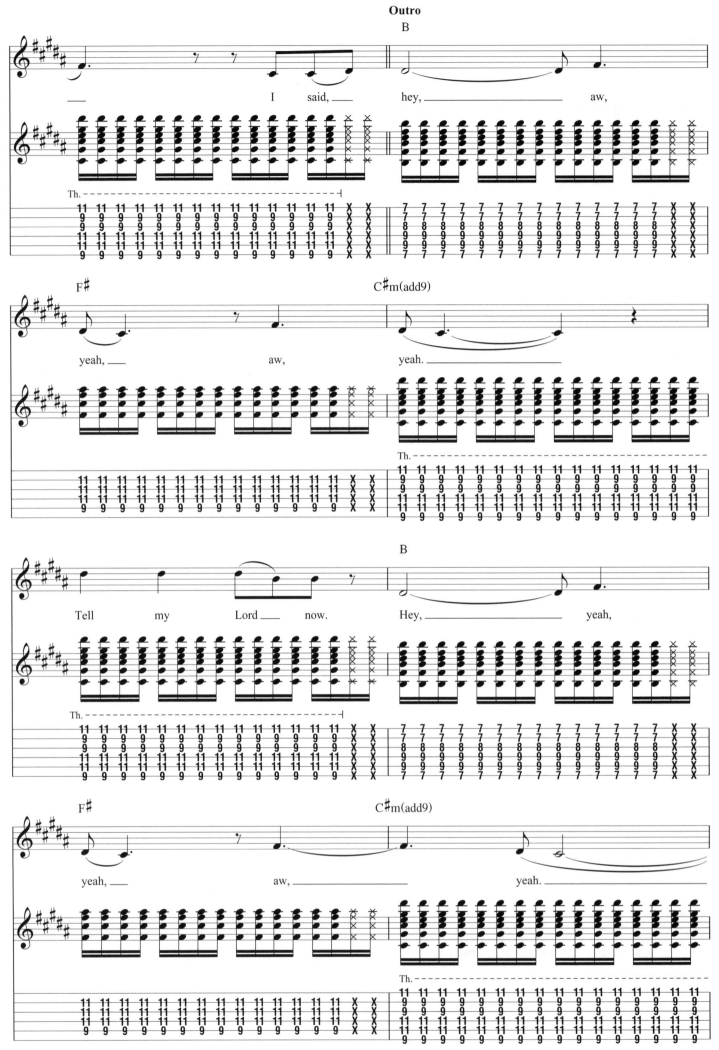

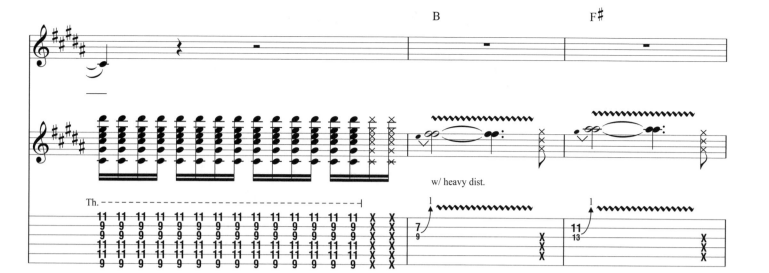

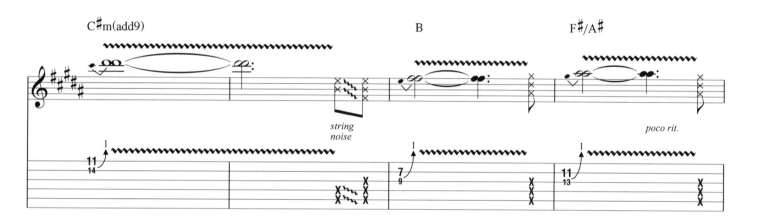

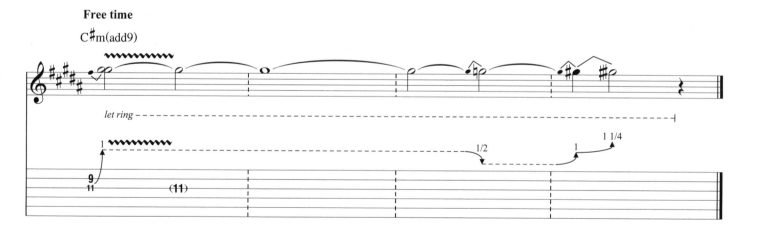

Additional Lyrics

2. When will I know that I really can't go to the well once more time to decide on?
   When it's killing me, when will I really see all that I need to look inside?
   Come to believe that I better not leave before I get my chance to ride.
   When it's killing me, what do I really need, all that I need to look inside?

3. When to descend to amend for a friend all the channels that have broken down?
   Now you bring it up, I'm gonna ring it up just to hear you sing it out.
   Step from the road to the sea to the sky and I do believe what we rely on.
   When I lay it on, come get to play it on all my life to sacrifice.

Tell Me Baby

Words and Music by
Anthony Kiedis, Flea, John Frusciante and Chad Smith

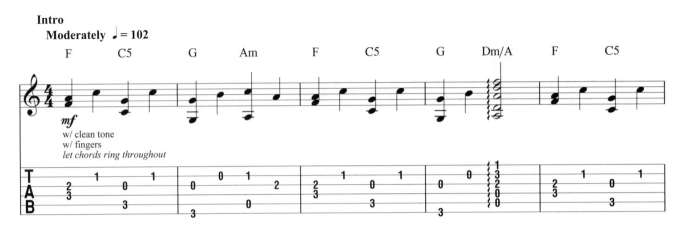

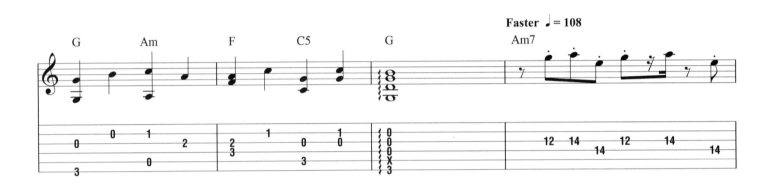

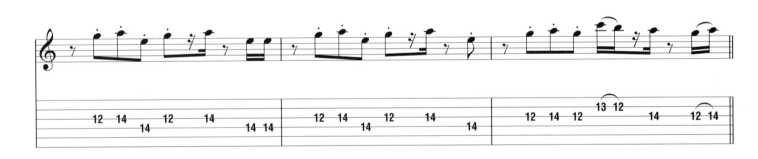

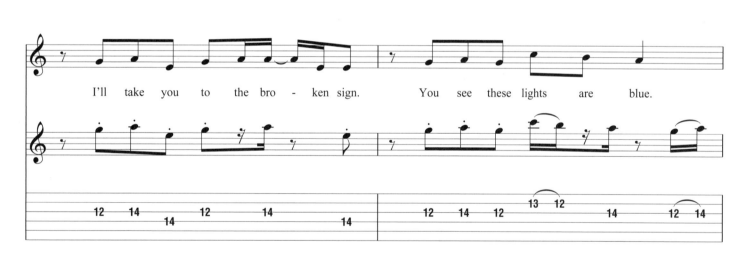

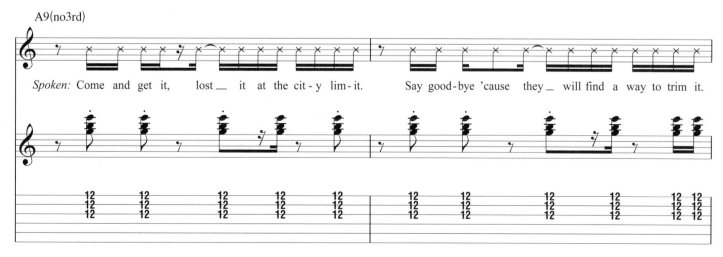

D.S. al Coda 1

Interlude

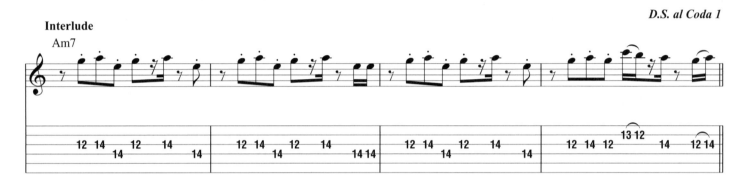

Coda 1

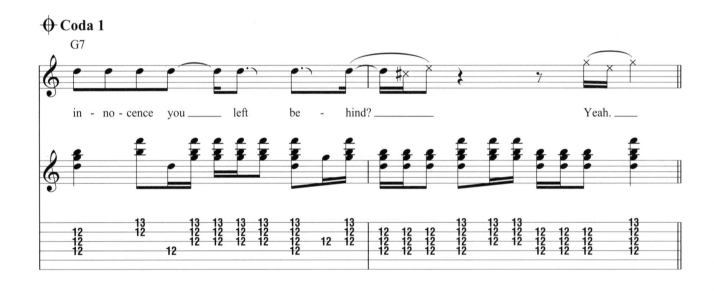

Guitar Solo

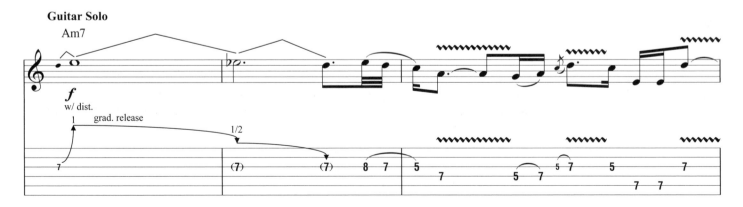

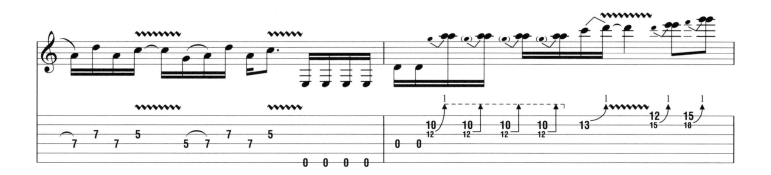

D.S.S. al Coda 2

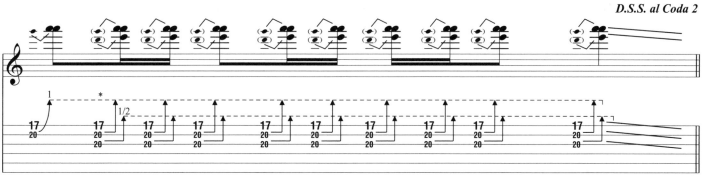

*Allow 3rd string to be caught under ring finger.

⊕ Coda 2

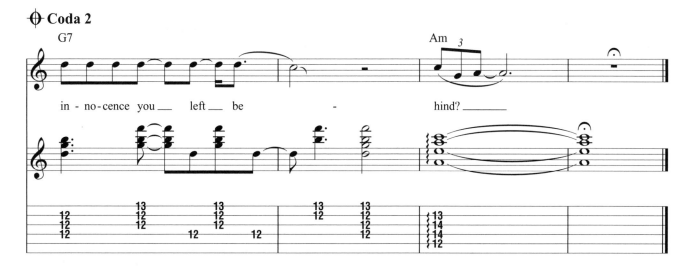

in - no - cence you __ left __ be - hind? _____

Additional Lyrics

2. Some claim to have the fortitude too shrewd to blow the interlude,
Sustaining pain to set a mood, step out to be renewed.
I'll move you like a baritone, Jungle Brothers on the microphone.
Getting over with an undertone. It's time to turn to stone.
Chitty, chitty baby, when your nose is in the nitty-gritty.
Life could be a little sweet, but life could be a little shitty.
What a pity, Boston and a Kansas City.
Looking for a hundred, but you only ever found a fitty.
Three fingers in the honeycomb, you ring just like a xylophone.
Devoted to the chromosome the day that you left home.

Under the Bridge

Words and Music by Anthony Kiedis, Flea, John Frusciante and Chad Smith

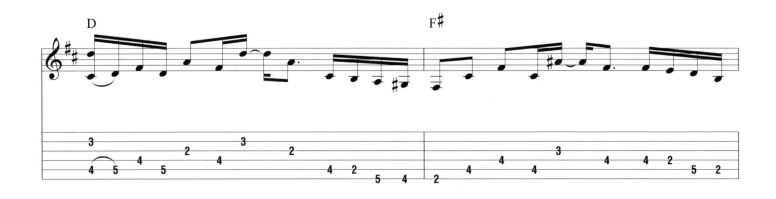

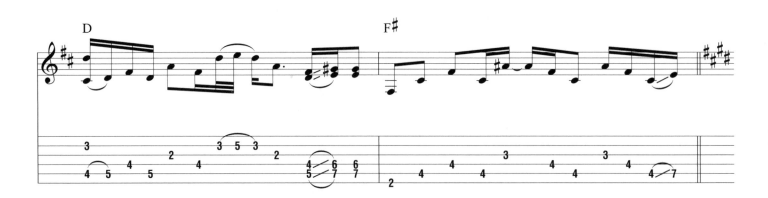

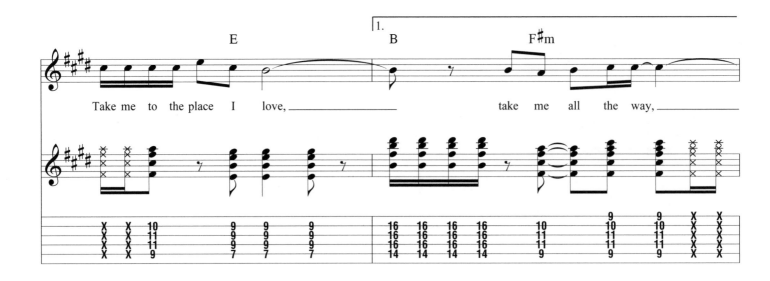

Take me to the place I love, _____ take me all the way, _____

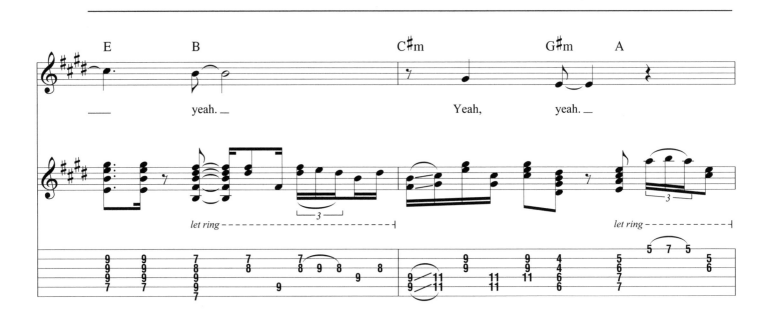

___ yeah. ___ Yeah, yeah. ___

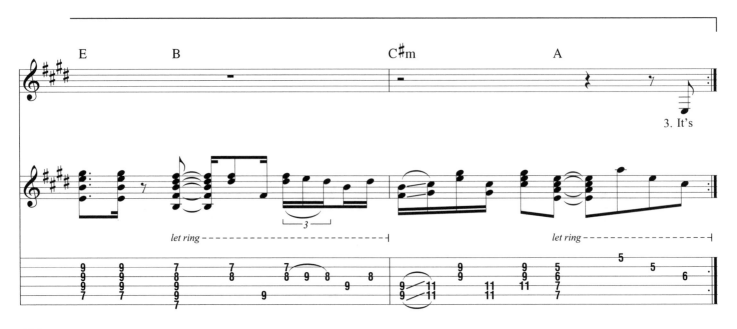

3. It's

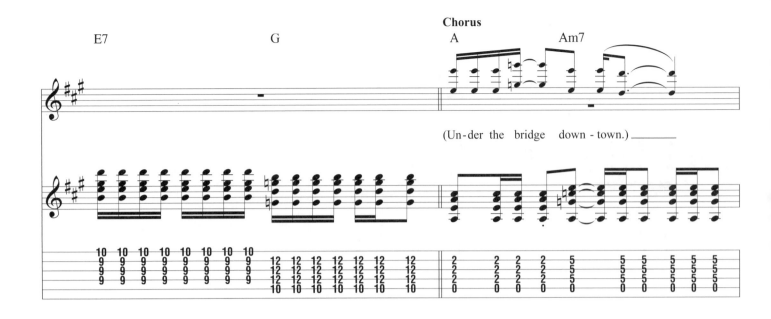

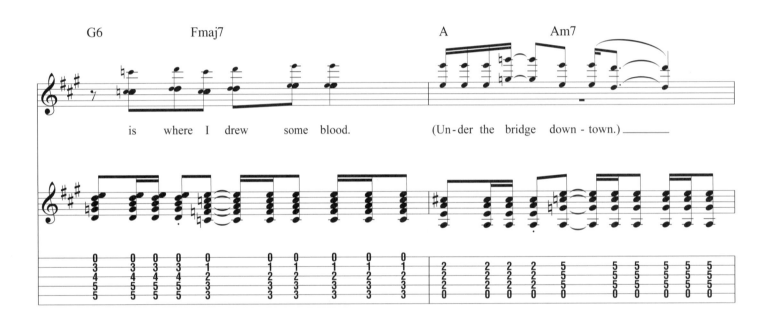

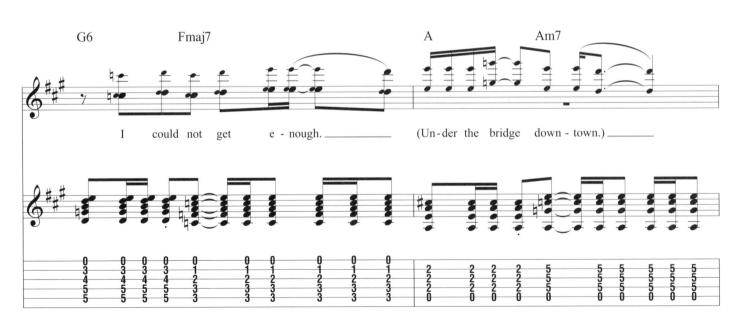

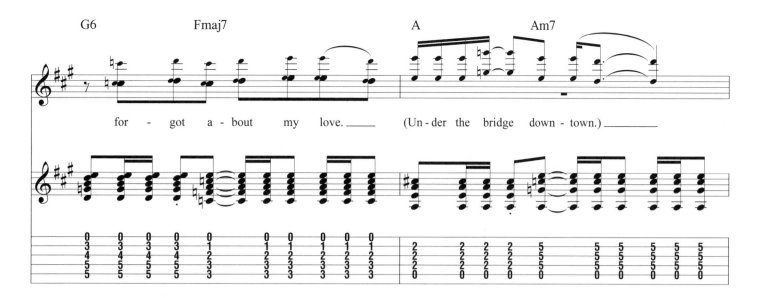

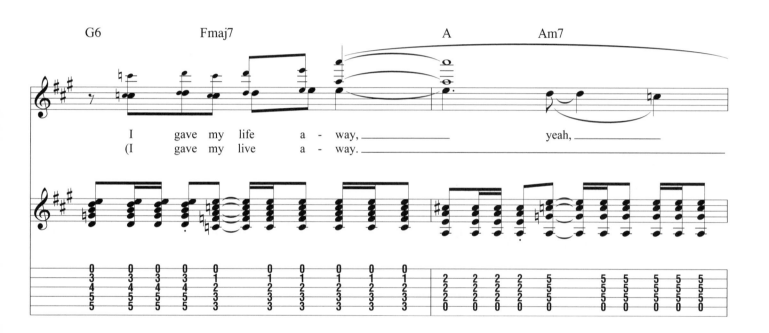

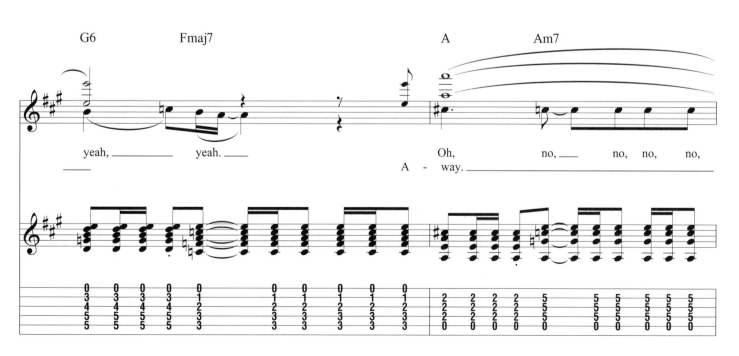

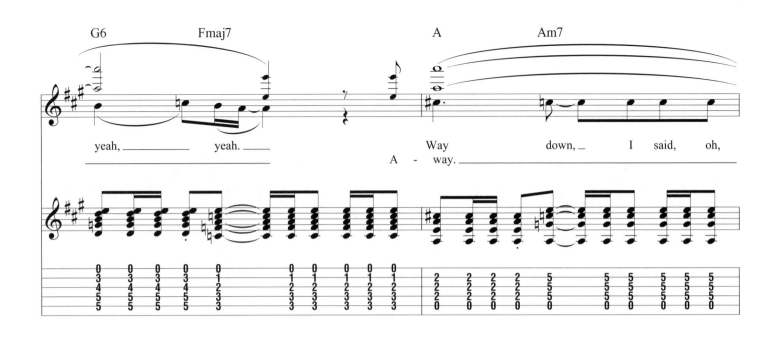

yeah, _____ yeah. _____

A - way. _____

Way down, _ I said, oh,

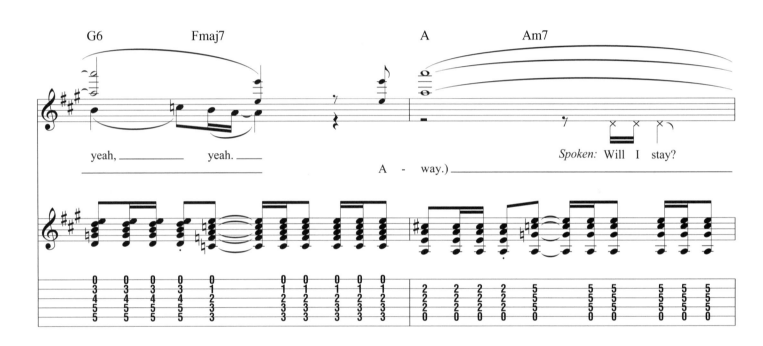

yeah, _____ yeah. _____

A - way.) _____

Spoken: Will I stay?

Outro

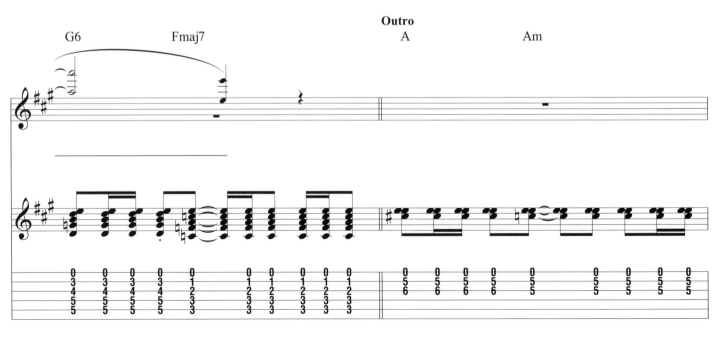

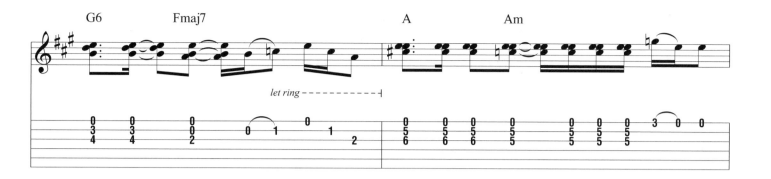

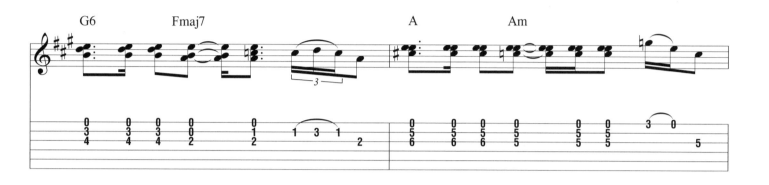

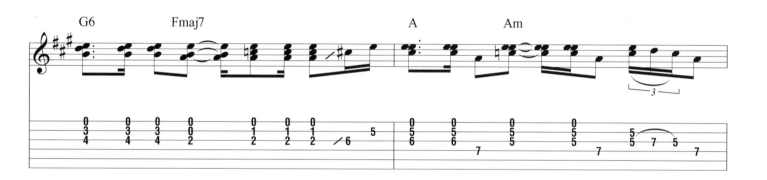

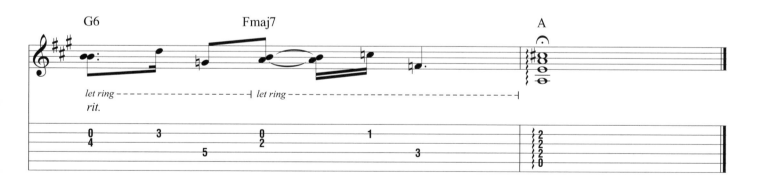

Additional Lyrics

3. It's hard to believe that there's nobody out there.
   It's hard to believe that I'm all alone.
   At least I have her love, the city, she loves me.
   Lonely as I am, together we cry.

The Zephyr Song

Words and Music by Anthony Kiedis, Flea, John Frusciante and Chad Smith

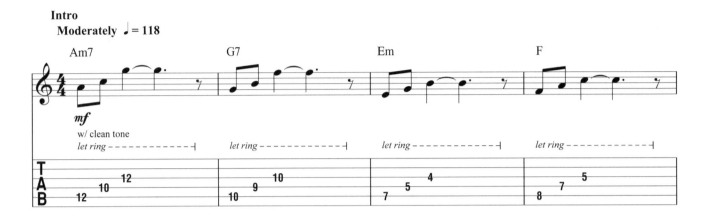

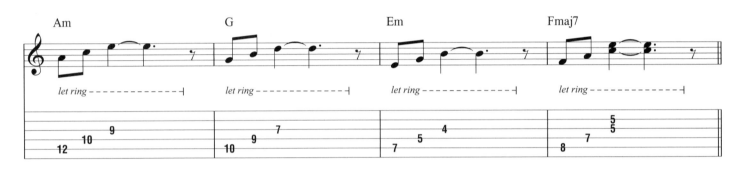

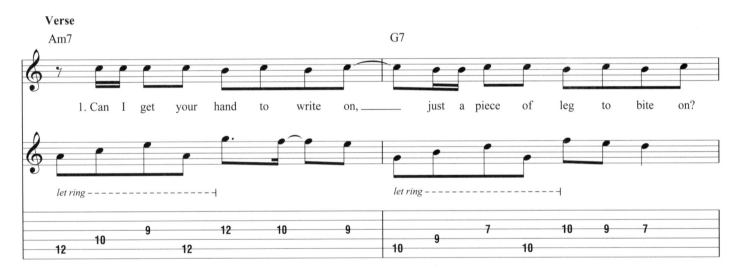

Guitar Solo

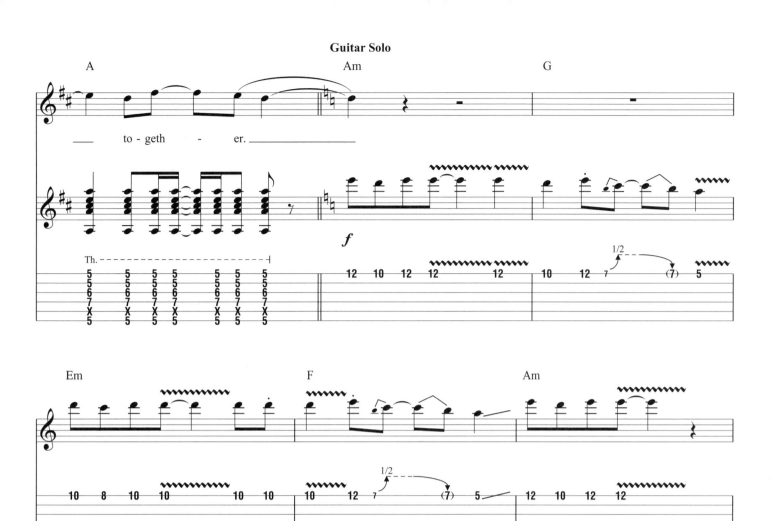

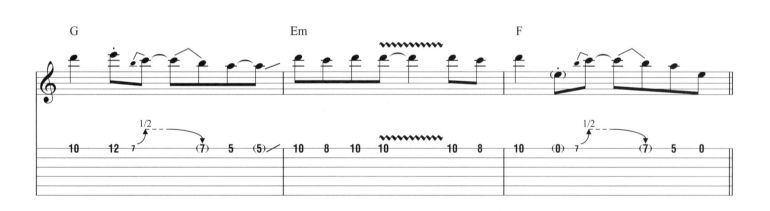

Bridge

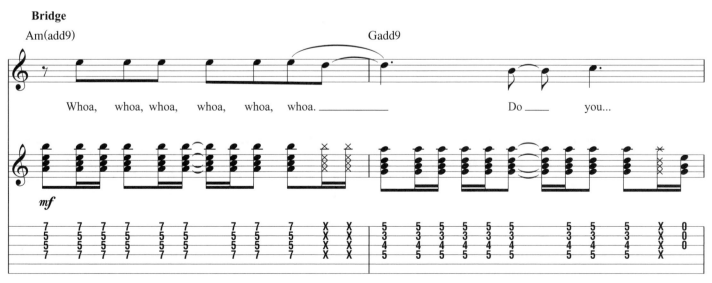

Whoa, whoa, whoa, whoa, whoa, whoa. _____ Do _____ you...

Outro

*w/ delay

*Set for eighth-note regeneration w/ 1 repeat.

For-ev - er.